THE ABC OF
THE ROCK GARDEN AND POOL

THE ABC OF GARDENING SERIES

THE A.B.C. OF THE ROCK GARDEN AND POOL

by

W.E. SHEWELL-COOPER

M.B.E., N.D.H., F.L.S., F.R.S.A., F.R.H.S., M.R.S.T.
Horticultural Diploma (Wye College, University of London)

Principal, The Horticultural Educational and Advisory Bureau
previously
H. Superintendent, Swanley Horticultural College
sometime
Horticultural Adviser, Warwickshire and Cheshire County Councils
Garden Editor, B.B.C. (North Region)
and
Command Horticultural Officer, South Eastern and
Eastern Commands, 1940–48

Published by
HODDER & STOUGHTON LIMITED
for THE ENGLISH UNIVERSITIES PRESS LTD.
LONDON

DEDICATED

with permission

TO

Major General Sir REGINALD DENNING, K.B.E., C.B.

Chief of Staff, Eastern Command,

who from

1943 to 1944

was my M.G.A.

in South Eastern Command

and

who was such an encouragement and help when we
were starting the Army Horticultural Training Centres.

First printed 1949

*Made and Printed in Great Britain for the English Universities Press, Ltd., London,
by C. Tinling & Co., Ltd., Liverpool, London, and Prescot.*

AUTHOR'S PREFACE

YEARS ago I was asked to write a book on Rock Gardens and another on Garden Pools—and I did so. I am glad to say they both sold well—but then the 1939 War came and it proved impossible to reprint them. So came the brainwave of amalgamating them into one book and including them in the A.B.C. series—and here they are—or it is!

I have had lots of people to help me as usual! Miss K. Beckh, Dip. Hort. (Swanley), of the Horticultural Bureau's staff is an Alpine specialist and has been most kind in helping with the excellent list of Alpine plants. Miss E. Kerr, who was trained at Studley, another of my assistants, worked hard with me on the lists of the various plants needed for the pool.

Mr. S. G. Boakes, A.M.I.Struct.E., the scientific expert of the Cement and Concrete Association, co-operated wholeheartedly with the chapters dealing with the use of concrete. I am most grateful to him.

Mr. Amos Perry, V.M.H., went through the original script on Pools, and Mr. L. Haig of Beam Brook, Surrey, made very kind suggestions *re* the " Collections " that might be used in the various pools. He has also seen the script. I am very grateful to both these experts.

Then I must thank Miss M. Walpole, B.Sc.(Hort.), who was on the staff of the Horticultural Educational and Advisory Bureau for her part, Miss M. Huntbach, N.D.H., for helpful criticisms and Miss G. Brydon, B.Sc.(Hort.), for originally correcting the proofs.

I am most grateful to Perry's Hardy Plant Farm and to Mr. H. Smith of Westcliffe-on-Sea for helping me with the photographs. I think you will agree they are very beautiful.
I do hope that my many friends will like this new addition to the A.B.C.'s and that they will help as usual by pointing out any errors that may by some mischance have crept in.

W. E. SHEWELL-COOPER,
Principal,

The Horticultural Educational
     and Advisory Bureau, Hextable, Kent.

CONTENTS

ILLUSTRATIONS

PLATES

7

CHAPTER I

THE REASONS FOR ROCK GARDENING

Do you want to know that—
1. Plants can be grown in a small place ?
2. It is easy to look after ?
3. It makes such a pleasant contrast ?
4. It gives colour all through the season ?
5. There is such wonderful variety ?

IT may seem peculiar to some people to write a chapter on the reasons for rock gardening, but there are many who have an idea that the reason for rock gardening is so that a large number of rocks can be used. I can think of a dear relation of mine who has made several rock gardens in her time, or rock gardens so-called, which seem to consist merely of a bank on to which a large number of odd pieces of brick-bats, marble, etc., have been thrown. Between these unnatural stones various plants are put in, and the whole thing looks most artificial.

A rock garden should be made to accommodate those plants that like growing under particular conditions. After all, there are hundreds of plants that have been collected from the Swiss Alps and from the mountains of India, China, Peru, and, in fact, from all over the world. These plants, growing at a high altitude, like particular surroundings. They may be covered with snow throughout the winter and then in the summer the sun may beat down upon them, for where they grow they are much closer to " King Sol " than in our gardens.

They are used to having plenty of icy cold water at their roots, and, though they are covered with snow, the cold is dry and they can live throughout frosty weather, whereas they often die miserably in the moist winters that they have to put up with in this country. As will be seen later, they may have to be given a certain amount of protection in the winter for this reason.

Another reason for rock gardening is that it is possible to have very large numbers of dwarf plants. They are small, and because of this a great many of them can be put into a confined space. They are free flowering and have among themselves some of the most glorious colours—and they can stand wind better than almost any other class of plants.

The rock garden, then, should be an attractive proposition for the small gardener as well as for those with quite a large area at their disposal.

A rock garden usually attracts womenfolk because it is comparatively easy to look after. It is slightly raised, or at any rate certain parts of it are, so that the necessary hoeing and titivation can be done without continual bending. As many of the Alpines like barren soil, weeds do not grow so luxuriously, but, in greater numbers, need hand weeding from among the plants. It is useful for the man or woman who finds it difficult to obtain organic manure, for, providing the pockets for the plants have been properly made up, they remain productive for many years without the addition of more humus-forming material. What top feeding is done can be in the form of special compost as advised on page 66.

Providing good weathered rocks are used, the rugged appearance of this form of gardening is also a special attraction. The flatness of the lawn and the rose garden is necessary and so, if one wants some pleasant contrast and a sense of height, depth and distance, the careful placing of the rocks will produce this effect. It is wonderful the way the rock garden can make a garden seem larger.

Some people complain that the disadvantage of a rock garden is that it is in flower and looking beautiful in the spring and then is dull for the remaining months of the year. This book will endeavour to show that it is possible to have a succession of flowers throughout the various seasons and so from early in the spring until late in the autumn this part of the garden can be an attractive feature.

It will be noticed that the term " rock garden " has been used throughout this chapter in preference to that of " rockery."

A waterfall adds interest to a water garden.

N.B. The Juniper on the left is 2 ft. high — and that will give a rough idea of the scale.

The rockery may be a mass of rocks while the rock garden can have few rocks, providing they are properly placed.

A rock garden need not, therefore, be expensive though the original cost may seem to be high ; for if this initial cost is spread over a period of years and compared with other forms of gardening it will be found to be a cheap proposition. The fascination of this side of horticulture is surely due to the daintiness of the baby plants and to the wonderful variety that it is possible to obtain. Once the rock gardening fever sets in an enthusiast is born, and this enthusiasm lasts for a lifetime.

The combination of the rock and water garden is natural since this so often happens in nature. The marrying of the two together is of course quite a simple matter. It is merely, so to speak, the leading of the one into the other. So often at the Chelsea Show you see the little stream wending its way down through the rocks, perhaps splashing over what looks a perfectly natural waterfall and then flowing on calmly and serenely over some shaley surface into a natural pool beyond. The word " natural " has been used on purpose for to have the formal pool, as described on page 129, would of course be a travesty. Such a pool will have an uneven outline and may be semi pear-shaped and in fact of any shape at all to fit in with the surroundings but it must not be square, rectangular, oblong or perfectly round. The drawing on p. 11 shows the kind of outline such a pool may have together with the way it " joins on " to the rock garden proper.

CHAPTER II

CHOICE OF SITE, ASPECT AND MATERIAL

Orders please—
1. Keep away from trees.
2. Use any natural slope.
3. Local stone may be used.
4. Learn from Nature.
5. Make your own rocks !

THE choice of the site for the rock garden naturally differs from garden to garden, but if it is borne in mind that it should be placed where the plants can be viewed to the greatest advantage and where they will get the maximum amount of sun (at least for most of them), some idea will be gained as to the place in which this garden should be made. To make a rock garden in the shade of a tree is criminal and the Alpines planted there will just wither and die. Not only is such a spot sunless, but the soil round about is robbed by the roots and so is poor. But probably the most serious danger to the plant is that caused by the drip, drip, drip of moisture from the branches and the falling of dead leaves in autumn. It cannot be over-emphasized that many Alpines very much dislike the damp English winters. The additional drips from the branches of trees would certainly mean death. Collections of dead, soggy leaves round the plants would cause them to rot off, if not continually cleared away, and this of course means a great deal of extra work.

As a rule the rock garden should not be near the house, although there are exceptions where a rock garden slopes up to the south side of a house built of local stone.

If there should happen to be any undulation in the garden and the place is sunny, this spot is ideal, for the rocks can be placed there and height and depth attained without artificiality. A low spot is sometimes chosen because it is the only suitable place, and if it is, then perfect drainage should be carried out.

This may mean filling in with large clinkers to a depth of 18 inches to 2 feet and in addition, a certain amount of agricultural pipe drainage may be necessary to carry the excess moisture away.

If there is to be a path down the rock garden it can traverse naturally along the lowest plot. Some excavation might be necessary in order to give the right effect ; if this is done the plants are more easily seen as they grow happily between the rocks on either side of the path.

Where the garden is small and there is no definite depression, a mound with varying contours may be raised to the south side, with a path skirting its irregularly shaped outline.

The site should really be where the rock garden can be made a separate feature. A narrow bed of flowering shrubs may be used as a division, or the garden may be screened in some other way, and though this is not a necessity, it does mark a division between the rock garden and the rest of the garden enabling the gardener to fit it into the general scheme informally.

The rock garden should be as natural as possible, and in a moderate-sized garden it would be a mistake to place it near the formal beds, or even in sight of them. These two features have nothing in common. In smaller gardens, where perhaps there is no room for " a proper rock garden ", the herbaceous or shrub borders may be edged with rocks with Alpines planted in pockets between them.

It must be remembered that although an open aspect is desired, some plants revel in full sun, while others prefer a cool, partially shaded spot, and these various aspects may be obtained by the careful placing of the rocks themselves.

As I said elsewhere, " It is not everyone who can afford to buy rocks brought from long distances." It is very nice to have beautiful weather-worn limestone from Somerset or Westmorland. The water and weather-worn limestone from Derbyshire and Cumberland is also very attractive, in fact most of the prize-winning rock gardens at the Chelsea and Southport Shows are made with such stone.

Use of Grass in Rock Garden to give a Permanent green introduction. Note paving at the edges to allow mowing.

A visit to the counties where the outcropping of these rocks appears is always an education, and teaches the prospective rock-garden maker how his more miniature effort should be " built."

Those who live in the county of Kent may prefer to use the Kentish rag, while in Surrey and Sussex there are many rock gardens made with the sandstone found in those counties. Harder stones, like granite, are sometimes used by those living in Wales, and in Devon or Cornwall, but the harder stones do not absorb moisture like the softer ones and so do not encourage plants to cling to them. Softer outlines can be obtained with limestone than with the more rugged rocks of granite.

It may be advisable to make the rock garden with the stone found in the district. In the first place it will be cheaper, and secondly, it may look more natural. If this is done, it is better for the stone to be dug out of the hillside, almost intact, than for it to be quarried out of the bowels of the earth. The stone that is on the surface has been weathered, and so shows the markings of water and the original geological outlines. These help to give the natural appearance and, incidentally, make it easier to build up the garden in the way Nature would like.

Stone that is quarried cannot fail to have a newish appearance and is more difficult to lay in the soil in a natural formation. It has, however, been used on many occasions with great effect because the designer had vision and could see what would look right and natural. The best side of the rock should always be visible and the unnatural looking quarried edges should be hidden beneath the soil. All stones have to be set quite deeply and so this should be easy to do.

When buying stone, the fact that three-quarters of the bulk of each one of them will never be seen should always be borne in mind. It is so easy to look at the rock as a rock exposed and away from its natural surroundings and not to see it properly placed in position, with only a small portion of it, perhaps in view. Stone that has been used lately is Tufa, a somewhat soft stone which occurs in some parts of the country. Curiously enough it is used in the construction of much of the crypt at Rochester Cathedral. It is impossible to list the names of all stones that have been used in constructing rock gardens.

The main thing should be to use stones with a massive appearance, even if there are only comparatively few of them, rather than a larger number of smaller ones. For the bigger garden, there should always be two stones at least that weigh half a ton each, with the remainder weighing, say, three hundredweights each. For quite small rock gardens, the two main stones should weigh five hundredweights, and the others one hundredweight each. It is difficult to be dictatorial but this is a plea, for the use of " rocks " rather than " stones."

Latterly, those who are unable to purchase rocks have tried making their own by means of concrete. The method adopted is to dig a large irregular hole of the shape required and, of course, of the size. The bottom of the hole should be sprinkled with sand or brickdust, or any other material that will give the surface of the rock the colour and texture desired.

The following mixture of concrete is then used : one bucket of loose cement, four buckets of damp sand and five-eighths bucket of water. The sand and cement should be mixed together first, and the water should be added gradually. The amount of water mentioned should just be enough to give a really stiff concrete mix. This should be placed in the hole, embedding in the centre for lightness and economy, old jam pots, tins, etc., making sure that these are well covered with the concrete. The surface should be finished as required and sand sprinkled on top.

This idea of filling the centre of the rock with jam jars and tins is a good one, for though the rocks have plenty of bulk they are not too heavy to move about or place in position.

The rock should be left to harden in its hole, and this usually takes two or three days. It may then be dug out carefully and the surface can be altered somewhat—if it is really necessary—by scoring it with a trowel.

Another method of making these artificial stones is to dip large pieces of slag or broken breeze slabs into a mixture of neat cement and water.

A tub is half filled with the mixture, which should be of a creamy consistency, and pieces of slag are then immersed in the mixture and allowed to remain there for a few seconds to permit the grout to penetrate the slag.

It is also possible to build up large boulders in this manner by bedding the pieces of stone on top of one another.

The main drawback to concrete rocks is that it takes some time for them to weather. The rapid growth of lichen will be encouraged if the surface of the rock, when dry, is painted with liquid cow manure or a mixture of flour, milk and water. In a few weeks, it will probably be difficult to distinguish home-made stones from natural stones.

It is not easy to make a large natural-looking rock at the first attempt, but amateurs have done it with great success. They have been able to improve on my suggestions by putting in irregular shaped material in the bottom of the hole so as to give the appearance of stratification and weathering. At least one man bought one or two stones and then used them to make earth moulds into which he could cast the cement and so produce others of a similar size and shape. The disadvantage of this scheme was that the rocks in the garden looked too similar.

To sum up : (1) The rocks should look as natural as possible. (2) They should be as large as possible and yet in proportion with the garden. It is often quite " right " for them to be of the stone natural to the district. (3) A great deal depends upon the setting.

CHAPTER III

MAKING THE ROCK GARDEN

Questions for you—
1. Think before you start !
2. How does nature do it ?
3. Will you start at the bottom ?
4. Please what is a stratum ?
5. Does it look natural ?

WHOLE books have been written on the subject of making the rock garden, for the actual placing of the stones so that they may represent natural rock is one of the most important parts of the work. Few people want to build up a rock garden this year and pull it down the next, when it is made it is made for good—or at least for a number of years.

It is, therefore, of great importance to give much thought to the placing and layout even before the stone has been ordered or a spade has been put into the soil. In the previous chapter reference has been made to the importance of going out to study mother nature, and how important this is. I have often been for drives in the Cheddar Gorge to see the natural outcropping there. I have wandered among the dales of Yorkshire and over the hills in Derbyshire and again, with eyes to see, dame nature has been an efficient mistress. The more skilled the builder of the rock garden, the more natural will it look and furthermore the less rock proportionally will be used and yet with much better effect.

The builder with his red bricks has to learn about English and Flemish bonds when arranging his courses, and the maker of the rock garden must learn about stratification and the laying of stones at the right slope. The pockets where the plants are to grow must be provided in the places where nature provides them herself and that is on the back, at the sides and below the rock, as well as in the area in between where the rain may have deposited a layer of fine soil and semi-decayed organic matter over some rock which lies beneath.

19

The man who builds a rock garden must be able to see the end at the beginning, he must have a reason for its starting and an equally good reason for it leaving off. The picture must be complete. It is no good trying to thrust the rock garden of the mountain into a small garden, the gardener must have the whole perspective in mind and somehow his innermost being will tell him how big or how high, how wide or how long his rock garden should be.

One gets far better ideas for the home rock garden by studying the small outcrops one sees on hillsides, than by looking at some massive cliffs. It is from such natural outcropping that the meaning of the word stratum may be understood as applied to the rock garden. Even then stratification should not be overdone and rigid lines emphasized in consequence, strata in nature often consisted of bands of rock of the same thickness originally but owing to the uneven durability of the stone or to some upheaval the plainness of the line has been broken up and several bold blocks may easily appear within the strata. Sometimes the density of the deposit varies, after all the course of stratification is the depositing done by water thousands of years ago and presumably the material had time to dry year by year and so you have the matter being built up as if piles of slates were laid one upon the other somewhat unevenly. Follow this by an upheaval caused by an eruption or an earthquake and the piles of slates can be split unevenly or be upended or torn asunder. But despite these happenings the lines of stratification always appear, there may be so to speak the primary line showing how and where the original material was deposited and there may be the secondary lines caused by the upheaval whatever it may have been.

As has already been suggested the depths of the layers would vary either because of the unevenness of the depositing or because of the subsequent wearing away by wind or water. In a similar way the depth of the stone used for our rock garden can vary from say one foot to five feet when building up the general lines of the stratum we feel will suit the

ARRANGE THE ROCKS NATURALLY
(NO HARD OR STRAIGHT EDGES)

picture in hand. It is useful to start so to speak with the idea of forming a miniature hill and to use for this purpose the biggest piece of stone available in order to convey the impression of height, rather than actually building a high mound. It is not necessary, however, to start with a mound or sloping soil for building, for the lower stones when placed in position may give the necessary *hint* of greater height and so soil may be brought to that point. It is always necessary to start at the lowest part of the rock garden and to bed the lower rocks in their right strata, or to put it another way, at their right angle, well into the ground. They should be put in sufficiently deeply to make them look like a natural outcrop and they thus incline towards the main bed of soil in which they rest. The backward slope of the big rocks used helps to get the rain down to the roots of the plants and not to take it away from them. Other rocks will then be placed in position and the " tilt " will either be to the right or to the left, the general slope of the strata being followed when placing the other rocks, and so the small garden will be made with one general indicative slope but with the occasional glimpses of the upheavals that occur in nature, thus causing vertical joints, many of them running parallel to each other and perhaps parallel to the face of the rock.

The rock garden therefore is to be regarded as the natural range of outcropping in miniature. Therefore, before placing the stones in position ; look at them carefully and see if there are any particular markings. These may well determine where the stones are to be placed, look at the graining and the weather markings and watch for the colours, and then try to blend these one into the other so that they become naturally part of the whole. Stones with really well-marked grainings are much easier to lay in position I always think, than rocks like the harder limestones or granite, in which the marks do not stand out. It is important, therefore, not to move the rocks about too much on soil or otherwise they get stained or muddied up, and then it is not so easy to recognize the markings and to fit them into the picture.

WINTER PROTECTION for a delicate rock plant.

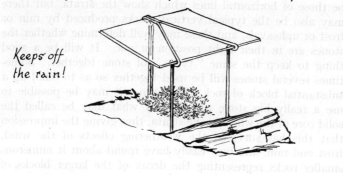

Keeps off the rain!

SECTIONS OF GOOD ROCK WORK.

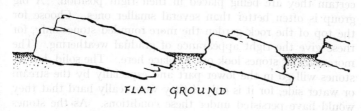

FLAT GROUND

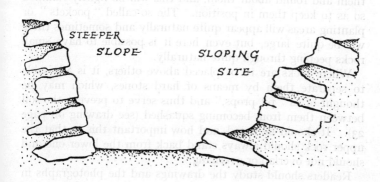

STEEPER SLOPE

SLOPING SITE

As has already been suggested, the markings may not only be those of horizontal lines which show the strata, but there may also be the typical vertical marks produced by rain or frost or upheavals, and these may well determine whether the stones are in their right position or not. It will be a good thing to keep the same " types " of stone together. Sometimes several stones will be used together so as to build up a substantial block of rock, other times it may be possible to use a really big stone to represent what may be called the solid core of the whole of the strata, thus giving the impression that this has survived the weathering effects of the wind, frost and rain, and may easily have round about it numerous smaller rocks representing the decay of the larger blocks of stone that were once its neighbours.

Having taken the utmost care, study the rocks to make certain they are being placed in their right position. A big group is often better than several smaller ones. Choose for the top of the rock garden the more rounded stones only, for these give the right appearance of gradual weathering. The more angular stones look out of place here. The solid, harder stones will go in the lower part and especially by the stream or water side, for it is only if they were really hard that they would have persisted under these conditions. As the stones and rocks go into position, suitable soil will be placed behind them and round about them, and this will be tightly rammed so as to keep them in position. The so-called " pockets " or planting areas will appear quite naturally and sometimes these will be quite large, but even here it is possible to have small rocks peeping through quite naturally.

Where rocks are to be placed above others, it is advisable to separate them by means of hard stones, which may be thought of as " pit props," and thus serve to prevent the soil between them from becoming squashed (see drawing on page 23). It should be noted, and how important this is, that the upper rock should always stand back from the lower one and should not overlap or overhang.

Readers should study the drawings and the photographs in

this chapter and others, which will perhaps give them a better idea of what a natural garden should look like than any written description. At the risk of boring the reader (and I should hate to do this), may I repeat that it must look natural. I say this because I have seen so many rock gardens that look quite unnatural. Again and again I am taken to admire a mound of soil with a lot of stones jutting out of it, looking like almonds peeping out of a trifle, very often hideous marble stones are used or brick-bats or even clinkers. The wrong way to place stones is to have them sticking out higgledy-piggledy anywhere without any thought being given to the natural placing of the rocks.

It is impossible to study detail too much even when one has looked at nature, and even when the book has been read and studied, it is indeed possible to allow some trifling mistake to appear which somehow upsets the whole atmosphere of the rock garden and makes it look quite unreal. By the way, note when looking at nature's efforts, to see how often you get your rocks in pairs, one sometimes being smaller than the other, very much like the sheep and her lamb.

ROCK FRINGED GARDEN STEPS

Showing
small plants growing between steps
(Covering risers rather than steps)

CHAPTER IV

MAKING THE ROCK WALL AND LAYING CRAZY PAVING

Here we learn that—

1. Different levels provide interest.
2. Walls make good homes for plants.
3. You must leave space for plants.
4. Crazy paving suits the rock garden.
5. Special plants may be used for—— ?

IT is seldom that one finds an absolutely level garden and even when one does it is advisable, from the point of view of design, to try and ensure at least two levels. It makes the garden so much more attractive. Great interest can always be assured by accentuating the difference between the levels in the making of a rock wall, which will later be well furnished with suitable plants (a list will be found on p. 29). The bank between two terraces is also made into a wall garden, the steps from the top to the bottom terrace even being clothed with plants growing in between the cracks.

The rock wall may be a retaining wall, built against the bank and the soil behind it will keep it moist and will provide an extensive cool root run for the plants. Sometimes special rock walls, frequently called " dry walls ", are built to serve as a division between two parts of the garden taking the place, as it were, of the hedge. In this case, the soil dries out more quickly, and so plants which will tolerate dry conditions must be used for furnishing it. In both cases the soil must be free from weed roots, for when these are present the weeds will undoubtedly work their way through the rocks and so cause trouble in the years that are to come.

Varying types of stone may be used for building such a wall, but the best are undoubtedly the fairly flat rough stones which are 3 inches to 8 inches thick. These should be laid one on top of the other, the spaces in between being packed

27

firmly with a compost similar to that mentioned on page 34. Large enough cracks should be left to accommodate the roots of plants without cramping them too much. The stone should always be laid at a slight slope so that the rain water is allowed to drain down to the roots of the plants instead of dripping off the surface, and so as to prevent the stones at the top falling out of position.

Most people like to have a solid base so as to ensure that there is no chance of sinkage, and thus they lay the first two courses of rock work in cement and wait until this has set properly before completing construction of the wall. The face of the wall itself can slope slightly backwards, especially in the case of the retaining wall, because if it is built vertically, the weight of the soil behind tends to force it forwards, the angle of course need only be very slight. It is always better to do the planting as the building of the wall proceeds, so decide upon the plants that are to be used before you start, and make certain that you have them on the spot ready when the construction of the wall is commencing. The roots can be spread out properly, good soil can be used to fill in the spaces and thus no harm will come to the tender roots.

It is a good plan to try and arrange a successive display, starting for instance with the Aubrietias and yellow Alyssum and continuing on with the Helianthemums, some of the Campanulas and ending up, say, with Sedum Sieboldii.

FURNISHING AN OLD WALL

In some gardens brick walls or old stone walls have already been built and these may well be made more attractive by filling in the larger cracks and crevices with a good compost such as is advised on page 34, and rock plants can be grown in these. It is sometimes possible also to make cracks with a hammer and chisel on purpose. In addition, the tops of dwarf walls can be made into small strip beds sometimes by the judicious use of stones and bricks, a good soil mixture being placed in position to a depth of about 6 inches. I have known quite good effects occur just by sowing seeds of some of the neater growing annuals in cracks in the walls, and the following annuals are quite suitable : candytuft, brachycome, cheiranthus, Dianthus Heddewigii, eschscholtzia, Felicia Bergeriana, linaria, nemesia, ursinia.

PLANTS TO USE

The following is a list of plants which you can use in your rock wall. Make a choice of these. You will find full details with regard to them in the list given in Chap. XI, see pages 78 to 125. Again may I remind you to make certain that the plants you choose cover as long a flowering period as possible, and either make up your mind to have a complete range of colours, i.e. red, pink, yellow, purple, blue, white, rose, orange and lilac, or else if you prefer, plan to have a wall of one colour only.

Name of Plant	Colours	Flowering
Aethionema vars.	Pink and white	April–August.
Alyssum vars.	Yellow	April–July.
Arabis vars.	White and pink	April–June.
Armeria	White, pink and red	May–August.
Aubrietia	Blues, mauves and reds	April–May.
Campanula vars.	Blues and white	May–September.
Cerastium	White	May–June.
Cheiranthus vars.	Orange, yellow and lavender	April–July.
Corydalis	Yellow	July–September.
Dianthus vars.	Reds, pinks and white	June–August.
Dryas	White	June–August.
Erinus	Red, pink and mauve	June–August.
Erodium vars.	Red, yellow and pink	June–September.
Erysimum	Yellow and lilac	April–July.
Gazania splendens	Orange	June–September.
Geranium vars.	Reds, pinks and white	June–September.
Gypsophila vars.	Pink and white	June–August.
Helianthemum	Red, pink, yellow, flame, etc.	June–August.
Hippocrepis	Yellow	June–August.
Hypericum vars.	Yellows	July–September.
Iberis	White and mauve	April–June.
Linaria vars.	Mauve, pink and white	June–September.
Lithospermum prostratum	Blue	May–September.
Nepeta	Blue	June–August.
Onosma vars.	Yellow and white	June–September.
Phlox vars.	Pinks, mauve and white	May–June.

Name of Plant	Colours	Flowering
Polygonum	Pink	August–September.
Saxifraga vars.	Red, pink, yellow and white	April–August.
Scutellaria	Violet	July–August.
Sedum vars.	Yellow, pinks and white	June–August.
Sempervivum	Yellow and reds	July.
Silene vars.	Pinks and white	May–August.
Thymus vars.	Pinks, mauves and white	June–August.
Tunica	Pink	June–September.
Veronica vars.	Blue and pink	June–August.
Zauschneria	Orange flame	August–September.

LAYING CRAZY PAVING

Of course flagged paths and crazy paving are useful in other parts of the garden beside the rock garden. It does, however, seem just right to have a stone path leading to the rock garden from perhaps the lawn or through, say, a little wild garden. The charm of these paths (in addition to the pleasing nature of the stone used) lies in the fact that there are many dwarf rock plants which can be grown between the stones, and most of them do not object to a certain amount of treading on. They must not, however, be laid just to resemble street paving. Too often a building contractor is given the job and he gets on with it, filling the joints in between with cement, and the effect is not natural.

The stones should be arranged so that they are level, with their flat surfaces upwards and with about an inch of space between them. The area for the path should be excavated and levelled evenly to a depth of at least six inches. Very often at the six-inch depth is laid a thin layer of coarse clinker or ashes or even stones, and on this an inch layer of sifted ashes may be placed. The surface should consist of the original soil which must be free from the roots of perennial weeds and be enriched with good horticultural peat at the rate of half a bucketful to the square yard, plus some fish fertiliser at the rate of four ounces to the square yard. Having raked this soil mixture level, the paving may now be laid in position.

It is a good plan to peg down tightly two lines running the length of the path parallel one to the other. If the path is to curve then pegs should be arranged close together, so that the lines may continue to be equidistant even though the path is to turn round a corner or " wave " slightly. The stones, when put down, should be made firm so that they do not rock when walked upon. The straight edges of the stones should be put along the line, so that the unevenness appears towards the centre of the paths, the edges remaining quite straight. The stones should be arranged quite level, and it is as well to have a builder's spirit-level available plus a fairly long plank, so that this may be assured.

Some people prefer the normal crazy paving; others like the more formal types of paving as are set out in the drawings on pp. 137, 138 and 140. As a rule, however, the crazy type of path is more suited to the rock garden and the more formal type of paving to the surrounds of a square or rectangular pool. It is easier to use the crazy paving too if the path is to wander about the garden.

As in the case of the rock wall, it is permissible to do the planting in the cracks of the crazy paving as the work proceeds, but there is a difficulty sometimes as a result of keeping the levels right. Some people purposely chip off corners of some of the stones so as to leave a space large enough to put in a plant. If, however, the plants go into position as the paths are being made, there is no difficulty at all in furnishing the path in such a way as to make it look very attractive indeed.

FURNISHING THE PATH

The types and kinds of plants used in the crazy paving are quite different from those used in the rock wall. The aim should be to use plants which do not mind being trodden underfoot. It is nice to have plants with scented foliage, and there are a number that fill this bill. When they are trodden on, aromatic perfume is wafted into the air. I refer to the creeping mints and the prostrate growing thymes in particular. There is at least one annual, with a very long name, Ionopsidium acaule, which looks particularly attractive when growing in between paving stones. It only grows half an inch high or so, and produces masses of pale mauve flowers. You only have to sprinkle the seed on the soil in the cracks early in April—very thinly—and it is not long before the plants are through.

PLANTS TO USE

There are plants of all kinds that can be used for growing in between crazy paving, some which only grow one inch high and less, and others which produce neat little tufts up to six inches in height. It is possible to arrange to have flowering plants of different colours, crimsons, pinks, blues, whites, purples, mauves and yellows, as well as plants with grey foliage, glaucous foliage, mottled foliage, marbled foliage, bronze foliage, scarlet and silver foliage and of course fragrant foliage.

All the plants need very little attention. Some of the taller growing ones will need an occasional thinning, or the removal of seeding heads, dead foliage or straggling stems. It is better to plant during the spring, when the Alpines will become established more quickly.

Mention has already been made of one annual that is particularly suitable for growing in between crazy paving, but the following plants may also be used if desired : the seeds are sown in late March and early April, where the plants are to grow and when they have finished flowering they should be removed. Many of them, however, conveniently seed themselves for the following year.

The plants I have used with success include Asperula setosa, azurea (12 inches high with numerous, sweet scented pale blue flowers) ; Clintonia pulchella (4 to 6 inches high with blue and white flowers) ; Leptosiphon hybridus (3 inches high with flowers of various colours) ; Virginian Stock (6 to 9 inches high, various colours) ; Sanvitalia procumbens (6 inches high with single or double yellow flowers) ; and Myosotis dissitiflora (9 inches high with large early flowers).

A rock garden showing miniature daffodils used to good effect with mossy saxifrages.

This photograph of an alpine house at Kew shows how you may have a wonderful display of flowers.

SUITABLE ALPINES FOR CRAZY PAVING

Name of Plant	Brief Description	Flowering Period
Acaena vars.	Glaucous or bronze leaves, red fruits	June–July.
Achillea vars.	White or yellow	May–September.
Ajuga	Blue	May and June.
Antennaria vars.	Pink and white	June.
Arabis	White	April–June.
Arenaria vars.	White and mauve	May–July.
Armeria vars.	Pinks and white	May–August.
Aubrietia vars.	Mauve to deepest red	April–May.
Bellium	White	Summer.
Campanula vars.	Blues and white	May–September.
Cerastium	White	May–June.
Cortusa	Bronzy green leaves	April–May.
Dianthus vars.	Reds, pinks and white	June–August.
Dryas	White	June–August.
Erinus	Mauve and red	June–August.
Frankenia	Pink	Summer.
Globularia	Blue	June.
Gypsophila vars.	White and pink	June–August.
Helichrysum	White and yellow	June–August.
Hieracium	Orange red	July.
Hypsella	White and crimson	June–July.
Linaria vars.	Purple and pink	June–August.
Lysimachia	Yellow	June–September.
Mentha	Mauve	June–September.
Oxalis vars.	White and yellow	Summer.
Phlox vars.	Pinks, lilacs and white	May–July.
Raoulia vars.	Silver and green leaves	
Polygonum	Pink	August–September.
Sedum vars.	White, yellow and pink	June–August.
Silene vars.	Pink and white	May–August.
Thymus vars.	Pink, red and purple	June–August.
Veronica vars.	Blue and pink	May–August.

CHAPTER V

SOILS, PLANTING AND PLANTS
FOR THE BEGINNER

Question Time :
1. What is a " well-drained soil " ?
2. Do plants have different needs ?
3. How shall I plant— ?
4. When is the best time to plant— ?
5. How do I plant— ?

Now we must consider the question of soils for the rock garden—naturally the ordinary person in the ordinary garden will make use of the soil that is already there, doing all that can be done to make it as suitable as possible for the usual run of hardy rock plants, and only making up special beds or " pockets " for those plants that are unlikely to thrive in the main section.

Time and again the phrase " a well-drained soil " is used. What exactly is meant by that ? It is by no means the same thing as a dry soil, but it does mean that the soil will not become dank and waterlogged during winter. This well-drained condition is assisted where the rock garden is elevated above the general level of the garden, but that alone is not always enough—the result is often nothing more than poor, dry soil.

The soil itself can be improved by the addition of various ingredients. Of these the most important is plant fibre of some sort. One of the best methods is to get a load of sods that have been cut, grass and all, from the top of an established pasture. These sods will be about 5 inches thick and should be stacked, grass side down, in a good square stack for about six months, by which time all the vegetation should be well rotted. Chop this " fibrous loam " into small pieces, about the size of a hen's egg, and mix it well with the garden soil. The presence of the fibre in the new loam will help to keep the soil open and therefore well drained, without being poor. The addition of coarse sand is also a good thing, but do not add too much as there is no plant food in it, and only those plants for which a specially sandy soil is recommended would benefit by the addition of more than one part of sand to eight parts of soil.

Details of the soil mixture for plants appreciating scree conditions are dealt with on page 39.

Some plants require a " lime free " soil, therefore in places where the natural soil is limey, it will be necessary to make up complete beds with lime-free loam and peat in equal quantities with one part in four of sand. Other plants such as Gentiana Farreri will thrive in a mixture of pure peat and sand. In all cases where a lime-free soil is needed, be sure that any covering in the form of stone chippings is also not limey, and any artificial watering should be done with rain water as far as possible, because places with a lime soil frequently have a water supply that also contains lime.

PLANTING THE NEW GARDEN

It is often convenient to plant a few of the larger features, such as the slow-growing conifers, at the same time as placing the rocks. These little trees are so much part of the framework of the design that their inclusion early in the proceedings helps one to picture the finished structure. Also it is possible to get the roots well down into the soil if done early, later on the job of digging a large hole for planting a shrub is difficult to do neatly.

Except for the large plants mentioned, it is best to delay planting until the soil has had time to settle. If the rock garden is constructed in autumn, delay planting until March or April.

Consider the placing of each variety, be sure you have some idea of the appearance of the full-grown plant before you put it in, then you will be able to put them in positions where they will be seen to best advantage. People are generally aware of the dangers of colours clashing if badly arranged, but one can have terrible "misfits" in size and habit of growth as well.

For positions where there is only a small amount of soil it is always best to plant young seedlings, in this way it is possible to get the plant well established while a large specimen would probably die of drought before it could get its roots down into the narrow cracks of rock.

WHEN TO PLANT

As a general rule, it is best to do planting in the rock garden in spring, even though that is very near the flowering time of some of the plants. Many small plants that grow quite happily planted in March would not have survived the winter if moved in November.

Another time when planting can well be done is during the late summer when many of the more rampant plants are being cut back and divided. This gives time for the newly divided plants to get well rooted in warm soil, and form neat hummocks before winter sets in.

Many nurserymen grow most of their Alpine plants in pots these days, and, provided the plants are well rooted and healthy, it is safe to plant them at any time, even in full flower, though if the weather is very dry it is best to give the hole a good " puddling " before turning the plant out of its pot and dropping it into the hole, and an occasional watering later will help it to get firmly established.

PLANTS FOR THE BEGINNER

Failure in the rock garden is a dismal sight, so the wise beginner will concentrate his energies on growing the obliging plants that are easy to grow, and he will thus be encouraged by his early success and rapidly leave the beginner's class and become a real enthusiast. There is a stupid kind of snobbery one meets, very seldom in real gardeners, that makes people want to look down on the cheery plant that co-operates with the grower, and will give a wholehearted display of colour, while they praise the sulky little plant that seems to grudge living at all, let alone giving more than an occasional bloom. Let us have none of that attitude, the garden that needs ruthless cutting back to avoid overcrowding is infinitely gayer in every way than the one that demands coaxing attention at all times, and lots of horrid little panes of glass scattered over it all winter !

The following are plants that will give a good display in the rock garden without preparing any special soils. Just the ordinary garden soil, treated as recommended earlier in this chapter, and as much sunlight as possible.

Name of Plant	Colours	Flowering
Achillea	White and yellow	May–September.
Alyssum	Yellow	April–July.
Anthemis	White	July–August.
Arabis	White	April–June.
Armeria vars.	Red, pink and white	May–August.
Aster vars.	Pink, mauve and blue	August–September.
Aubrietia	Blues, mauve, pink and red	April–May.
Campanula vars.	Blue, purple and white	May–September.
Cerastium	White	May–June.
Corydalis	Yellow	July–September.
Dianthus vars.	Reds, pinks and white	June–August.
Erodium vars.	Red, yellow and pink	June–September.
Geranium vars.	Reds, pink and white	June–September.
Geum	Orange, yellow and pink	April–September.
Gypsophila	Pink	June–August.
Helianthemum	Red, pink, yellow, white, flame, etc.	June–August.
Hypericum vars.	Yellow	July–September.
Iberis	White	April–June.
Nepeta	Blue	June–August.
Omphalodes	Blue	February–May.
Phlox subulata	Pinks, mauve and white	May–June.
Polygonum	Pink	August–September.
Primula Juliae vars.	Pink, purple and mauve	February–April.
Pulmonaria	Pink and blue	March–April.
Saponaria	Pink	June–August.
Saxifraga vars.	Red, pink, yellow and white	February–August.
Sedum vars.	Yellow, pink and white	June–August.
Silene Schafta	Rosy magenta	June–August.
Thymus vars.	Pink, mauve and white	June–August.
Veronica vars.	Blue and pink	June–August.

CHAPTER VI

THE SCREE, MORAINE AND STREAM

A scree not a scream !

1. What do I mean by scree— ?
2. The choicest plants need screes.
3. Make a scree.
4. Don't overplant.
5. Alpines don't like our damp English winters.

THERE has been a certain amount of argument as to the difference between a scree and a moraine. Most books seem to treat the two as one and use these two names alternatively. Actually, for the amateur, it is safer to regard the scree as the mass of rock debris and stones together with a certain amount of soil and sand maybe, which is brought down by the glacier and is left behind when this recedes. There are, of course, immense deposits of such material in the mountainous parts of Europe. The moraine, on the other hand, consists of similar material, but three feet or so below a water pipe will be laid and suitably punctured, so that a continuous underground stream of water can be provided at will. It is seldom, however, possible to do this today in view of the expense and lack of materials. Anyway it has not been found really necessary in this country, for it is very seldom, if ever, that the soil at that depth gets dried up.

We can therefore regard these two names as almost synonymous. However, in order to satisfy certain readers, I am purposely including a few notes on the moraine towards the end of the chapter.

THE SCREE

May I make it quite clear at the start, that it is only necessary to make a scree if you want to grow certain choice Alpines which will not thrive in ordinary rock garden soil. Many of the choicest plants must have perfect drainage, and, only flower at their best when they are growing in very little soil indeed. Do not make a scree and then grow in it the common plants that are perfectly happy under other conditions. Scree gardens are quite easy to construct and cheap to maintain and they may be made either on a slight slope or on the flat. A slope should never be too steep or the moisture may drain away too rapidly. If the scree is made on the flat, the bed should always be raised a little above the general level of the ground, about—say, 4 or 5 inches above.

As to the materials to be used in a scree, these should consist of a collection of small broken pieces of rock and plenty of chippings. Any kind of stone can be used, granite, mill stone grit, sand stone or even flint. All that is necessary is to dig out about two feet of soil and put into the hole thus excavated, big stones and rough material of any kind to provide drainage, smaller stones are used gradually towards the top with the finest ones on the surface. With the granite chippings or mill stone grit, a certain amount of horticultural peat, fine leaf mould and loamy soil may be used. Authorities seem to differ as regards the proportion, but a mixture consisting of 15 parts of fine stone to one of soil and leaf mould mixed together, would seem to be fairly common—and suitable. It is with the smaller stones which form the surface of the scree that this compost is mixed.

It is usual to select a sunny, slightly sloping site between, say, two bold rocks, so that the effect appears quite natural. The scree will then slope very, very gradually towards, say, a stream or maybe a further stratum of rock below. It would usually, however, be towards the base of the rock garden and will be fitted into the plan as the work of construction goes on, see chapter III. It is necessary to saturate the whole bed thoroughly as it is being constructed and to couple this with a good treading. Before the plants are put into position, all the soil should be shaken from their roots, so that these may be spread out shallowly in the fine scree material. The planting will be followed by a good watering, so as to help them to settle down.

Some people like to have the scree in the higher parts of the rock garden, so that the plants, when they are growing, will be flowering at the normal eye level. It is then possible of course to enjoy the effect at any time. As, however, there are plants which are lime lovers and which will therefore prefer a surface of limestone chippings in the scree, and also there are others which hate lime and so need granite and sandstone chippings, it is possible to provide more than one scree and so produce the right material for the various groups of plants to be grown. Naturally, in small rock gardens this is not possible, and the best idea under these circumstances is to have areas in the scree with limestone, while the bulk of the scree will consist of non-calcareous materials.

The great advantage of a scree garden is that very few weeds will grow there. The common garden weeds, such as groundsel and chicory, prefer a good rich soil and cannot flourish in the poor fare provided by the stone chippings. When a scree has to be quite small, it is usual to give it a little variation of surface in order to prevent it looking monotonous and flat. By the way, the watering given after the scree has been made tends to wash away the bulk of the soil at the surface and so leaves a nice layer of pure material on the top. It is quite a good plan to have an occasional large stone in the scree so as to produce a natural effect and in addition to provide stepping stones for getting about among the plants.

FURNISHING THE SCREE

Always plant the scree with young plants and preferably quite tiny ones. It is far more important to buy a plant with a really good root system and a small top than to buy what so many beginners seem to look for, and that is a plant with tremendous top growth and maybe poor roots below. The scree will be planted naturally. There will be no question of putting plants in in straight lines, there may be a little group here, a stray plant there, a drift of a glistening silver leaf plant towards, say, the edge, and so on. The planting must look natural and not spasmodic. It may be all right in nature, but extravagant gaps in the scree as found in Alpine regions, is overdoing it in the rock garden at home. Furthermore, most scree lovers will want to include a widely representative collection. On the other hand, don't overplant, and remember that the Alpines are going to spread—so give them room to develop. Bear in mind colour harmony and try not to have such arrangements as puce pink next to bright crimson.

PLANTS TO USE

In order to help readers decide as to which plants to use in the scree, a list will be found below giving brief descriptions and time of flowering. Further details with regard to these plants will be found in the more complete collections of plants given on pages 78 to 125.

Name of Plant	Description	Flowering Time
Acantholimon glumaceum	Light rose	June–July.
,, venustum	Rose	July–August.
Aethionema, all	Deep rose, pink and white	April–August.
Agathaea coelestis	Blue	June–September.
Ajuga crispa	Blue	June–July.
Alyssum idaeum	Yellow	May–July.
,, spinosum roseum	Pale pink	June–July.
Androsace, all	Pink and white	April–October.
*Anemone vernalis	Silvery white	March.
Antirrhinum Asarina	Yellow	May–September.
Aquilegia escalcarata	Brown purple	May–June.
Arabis Sturri	White	May.
Arenaria purpurascens	Lilac	June.
,, tetraquetra	White	May.
Armeria caespitosa	Pink	April.
Asperula, all	Pink and white	May–September.
Calandrinia umbellata	Magenta	July–September.
*Calceolaria Darwini	Yellow and red	July.
,, tenella	Yellow	May–September.
Campanula Allionii	Blue	June–July.
,, arvatica	Deep violet	May–June.
,, Bellardii vars.	White and blues	June–July.
,, Kewensis	Dark blue	May–June.
,, pulla	Purple	June–July.
,, Raineri	Blue	June–July.
,, Stansfieldii	Lavender	June–July.
Chrysanthemum Mawii	Pink	June–September.
Convolvulus mauretanicus	Blue	July–September.
*Cyananthus, all	Deep blue	July–August.
Dianthus Allwoodii alpinus Apollo	Pink	June–September.
,, Allwoodii alpinus Mars	Red	June–September.

B*

Name of Plant	Description	Flowering Time
Dianthus alpinus	Deep rose	June–July.
,, callizonus	Pink	June.
,, microlepis	Pink	June–July.
,, neglectus	Pink and buff	June–July.
,, superbus	White	June–July.
Douglasia Vitaliana	Golden	May–July.
Draba aizoides	Golden	March–April.
,, pyrenaica	Lilac	March–June.
Edraianthus serpyllifolia	Purple	May–June.
,, tenuifolia	Pale lavender	June.
Erigeron leiomerus	Violet	June.
Erinus alpinus and vars.	Various	May–August.
Eritrichium, all	Blue	June–July.
Erodium corsicum	Pink	June–September.
*Erythraea diffusa	Pink	June.
*Gentiana Farreri	Light blue	September–October.
,, verna	Blue	May–June.
Geranium argenteum	Rose pink	June.
,, napuligerum	Pink	June–July.
Globularia incanescens	Blue	June.
Helichrysum frigidum	White	May–August.
Hypericum empetrifolium	Yellow	June–September.
Hypsella longifolia	Purplish pink	June–September.
Iris cristata	Blue and gold	April–May.
Lewisia, all	Various	May–July.
Linaria alpina	Purple and pink	May–July.
Morisia hypogæ	Yellow	April–May.
Omphalodes Luciliæa	China blue	April–August.
Onosma, all	White and yellow	June–September.
Origanum Dictamnus	Rosy purple	July–September.
*Oxalis enneaphylla	White and pink	May–June.
,, lobata	Golden	June.
Papaver alpina	Various	May–September.
Pentstemon Roezlii	Ruby red	May–June.
*Phlox adsurgens	Shell pink	May.
,, Douglasii	Lilac	May.
Polygala, all	Various	May–August.
Potentilla nitida	Pink	June–July.
Primula marginata	Lavender	April.
,, pubescens	Various	May.
Ranunculus alpestris	White	June–July.
,, glacialis	White	June–July.
Raoulia, all	White silver foliage	July.
Saxifraga. Encrusted	White, pink and yellow	May–July.
,, Kabschia	Various	February–June.
,, Porphyrion	Lilac pink	March.
,, Engleria	Various	May–June.
Scutellaria japonica	Dark violet	July.
Sedum spathulifolium	Yellow	July.

Name of Plant	Description	Flowering Time
Sempervivum, all	Red, pink and yellow	July.
*Shortia uniflora	Pink	April–May.
Silene acaulis	Pink	June–August.
*Soldanella, all	Violet	March–April.
Statice bellidifolia	Mauve	July–September.
Thymus serpyllum coccineus	Red	July–August.
Verbena chamædryfolia	Scarlet	June–September.
Veronica Bidwilli minor	White	June.
Viola biflora	Yellow	June.

Plants marked with a star can only do well in a lime-free scree.

THE MORAINE

As stated earlier, on page 38, there is no real difference between the moraine and scree, except inasmuch, that it is usually accepted that in a moraine, water runs continually below the surface during the short period in spring and summer when growth is active. In nature this occurs because snow is continually melting and the water thus trickles down underneath the scree material. In the winter, of course, the ground is frozen and covered with snow many weeks but the plants are kept dry. They, of course, hate the damp winters we get in Great Britain and that is the reason that sheets of glass are often held in position above plants by means of what are called alpine clips.

The alpines that will not survive an English winter on account of dampness will thrive in the scree or moraine if they have a little glass protection above. This is particularly true in the case of the woolly leaved species. A moraine usually faces south and has a slope of, say, 1 in 16. It is made as a rule above a path, the natural conditions being imitated as nearly as possible. The underground irrigation of the moraine is said to be the nearest approach that any specialist has been able to achieve to the conditions found in, say, Switzerland. As a matter of fact, in Great Britain, nearly all the plants one wishes to grow do perfectly well in the normal scree without all the expense and worry of the underground watering system. As William Watson says in his *Gardener's Assistant*, "In truth under British conditions it is not essential though still of a value . . ."

CHAPTER VII

THE ALPINE HOUSE

Try one !

1. How about an Alpine House— ?
2. Such fun for the week-end gardener !
3. Equipment need not be large.
4. Alpines MUST have a good drainage.
5. Flowers all through the year.

THOSE who wish to grow alpines, and have not got the type of garden in which a rock garden is seen to best advantage, would do well to consider the possibilities of an alpine house. This provides great scope for the culture of many rare and beautiful plants, as well as many of the old familiar favourites which thrive equally well out of doors.

As a week-end gardener's hobby it is ideal, because much work can be done in winter under cover. It also gives an opportunity for appreciating many of the miniature flowers that are frequently overlooked when out in the rock garden among plants of a more flamboyant character ; seen in a small pan of their own, surrounded by small chippings of limestone, they become very important looking people, able to stand up to the scrutiny they would never receive out of doors. Many alpines flower very early in the year, at a time when there is little encouragement to go for a stroll round the garden just to see what is in flower, thus some of the most attractive of the saxifrages may open and fade without having been admired or commended for their bravery in facing the hard wintery weather of early February.

The alpine house can be small or large, and in either case, artificial heat is unnecessary. The two essentials are : plenty of light, and a watertight roof. The plants rely on their close, neat growth for much of their charm, and for this light is needed, while drips landing on the plants from a leaking roof is the surest way of killing even the sturdiest of them.

44

If the staging is made of wood slats, it must be given a solid covering of some sort. Sheet asbestos or corrugated iron will serve very well, and there should be a supply of drainage holes to allow surplus water to drain away. The best covering for the solid staging is stone chippings of some kind or gravel, this allows for an annual washing and prevents the accumulation of pests and weeds. Ashes are sometimes used, but are not nearly so satisfactory as the former, because they contain a lot of fine dust which settles down into a sticky mass which harbours worms and allows moss and weeds to grow.

On the whole, it will be found that pans look better than ordinary garden pots, as most of the plants will be low-growing and look ridiculously out of proportion sitting in the top of a pot some seven inches high. When stood on a gravel covered staging as recommended, the extra space for drainage provided by using a pot instead of a pan, is unnecessary.

It is possible to construct a small rock garden in a portion of the house, or use a stone trough or sink for the same purpose, in which the plants are grown as in the open. But in planting these, thought must be given in selecting the plants to be used, as many subjects benefit by spending part of the year (generally from after flowering until late autumn) out of doors, and naturally, this treatment is impossible for those growing in a bed weighing at least half a ton.

The potting equipment required will not be large. Pots and pans have already been mentioned, new pots always have to be soaked for a day or two and then air dried before being used, old pots need a thorough scrubbing, paying special attention to the ring of moss that generally forms on the inside at soil level. Crocks for drainage collect all too fast in most gardens. Fibre to cover the crocks will be got from the loam when it is sieved. The best way to manage the soils mixture problem, on the small scale needed for the private grower, is to keep a supply of the more usual ingredients in separate boxes or pails, and make up the special composts as required. The foundation ingredient is loam, this should be well rotted, by

A Beautiful Garden can be built in an old stone sink.

which is meant, that there is not any portions of living plants in it, yet the whole is still held together by the dead fibres of the grasses that were growing in it. Peat soil of some kind is needed, either in the form of the acid soil from a bog or as prepared horticultural peat. Leaf mould, made by stacking the fallen leaves of beech or oak trees, is a useful ingredient. Sand is of great importance, and it is surprising how difficult it is to get the best kind, sea sand is useless, pit sand has frequently too many fine particles in it, and therefore sets solid when watered, the best is river sand which is clean and sharp and promotes good drainage. A little crushed charcoal is often useful to add to a peaty soil when potting a plant that is likely to stay in the same pot for over a year, as it prevents the soil from going "sour". Sphagnum moss will be used occasionally, but is not essential; if cut up into small fragments and mixed with the other ingredients it helps to hold moisture when such plants as Soldanella are being grown.

Watering will be done as for other plants in pots, that is, plenty when it is needed and then left until it is getting dryish again. Never give small splashes, it is very bad for the plant.

When possible, have a frame filled with sand out of doors, and during the summer months the plants can be plunged into this, pot and all, until it is time to tidy them up and bring them in again. By having the pots embedded in sand up to their rims, the job of watering is much easier, as naturally, there is not so much evaporation, and the plants benefit by having their roots kept cooler.

The pots must have good drainage, and it is as well to look every now and then, to see that the holes have not got filled up with loose soil. Moss and weeds must be kept down, but this is greatly helped if the top of the pot is kept covered with a layer of stone chippings. As well as giving a neat appearance this is also advantageous in helping to keep the neck of the plants dry at watering time.

Very many plants can be grown in the alpine house, and it is as well to include a few dwarf conifers in pots to give an occasional block of evergreen among the other plants, but do not keep the trees if they get too tall to look nice, the miniature Juniperus hibernica compressa will stay a suitable size almost indefinitely, but if Cupressus Fletcherii is used to provide another shade of green, it will in all probability be getting too large after fifteen years.

If the list of plants recommended for screes to be found on page 41, is taken as a foundation for stocking the alpine house, it will provide a good selection from which to choose. Many others of the easier plants will also be useful to increase the display of colour, and the sedums, saxifrages and sempervivums, though not needing this treatment, will all do well in pots and give great satisfaction.

The pests and diseases should be few, aphis will be the most troublesome insect and spraying should be done as soon as the first one is seen. Among the diseases, mildews and moulds that attack the woolly leaved plants in foggy weather, are undoubtedly the worst, and for these, prevention in the form of careful watering, is better than any cure—though, keep a little Flowers of Sulphur handy to dust the plants, just in case.

CHAPTER VIII

FLOWERING SHRUBS, CONIFERS AND FERNS

Greenery is a change, so—
1. Use shrubs with discretion.
2. There are shrubs for colour !
3. Ferns, too, give an interest.
4. Something for the shady spot.

SHRUBS are very useful in the rock garden, not only because they provide a useful background for the alpine plants, but also because they give shade when this is necessary and protection. Furthermore, they are particularly effective in the winter time when so many of the normal alpine plants are not in bloom. Shrubs, too, improve the general look of the rock garden, but they must not be allowed to become too over-powering.

Shrubs, whether flowering or evergreen, should be used with discretion and where they prove most suitable, the number to be included will of course depend largely upon the size of the rock garden. Most of the shrubs recommended in the list at the end of this chapter are of a very dwarf character, others can easily be kept within bounds by the judicious use of a pair of sécateurs. Never plant a shrub that has to be kept clipped regularly as this looks far too formal. Some shrubs grow prostrate and so will screen a boulder, others are pointed and look like little pinnacles, some are evergreen, others lose their leaves in the winter, some have a round look, like little hedgehogs, and these are particularly slow growing and diminutive in character.

It is always as well to choose some shrubs for their berries, or for their autumn and winter colouring, and some for the intrinsic beauty of their flowers in the spring and summer. Some, like the Acer dissetum, have the most lovely, finely cut foliage which always reminds me of the plumage of some exotic bird. It is this group, by the way, that love to have plenty of peat worked into the soil for them. The baby rhododendrons also like plenty of peat and a soil which is free from lime. In the case of the smaller shrubs, don't put in a single specimen, try and get a real splash of colour, especially in the case of a large rock garden, but with the spire-like conifers—say, one of the Junipers, it is often possible to have one little sentinel alone, or perhaps one with a shorter friend beside him !

The deciduous shrubs (that is those that lose their leaves in the autumn) are best planted in the late autumn, but the evergreen kinds are usually planted in April, although in the south some people go in for September planting. Ordinary soil will suit most of them, and where special soil treatment is needed, details will be found under the heading " Remarks " in the list given on page 55.

LIST OF CONIFERS SUITABLE FOR THE ROCKERY

The list below gives the names of the most suitable conifers, but whilst some are dwarf by habit, others are only useful for the first 10-12 years or so of their life. Then they are too big to be good inhabitants of the rockery, and should be dug out. They are marked " O ".

ABIES balsamea nana. Has blue-grey leaves, and is like a dwarf fir. Its ultimate height and spread respectively are : 1½–2 feet, 2–3 feet. It has a low and spreading habit, and prefers a moist, shady spot.

CEDRUS Libani nana. Very slow growing, and of stunted habit. The young leaves are bright green. The maximum height is 2½–3 feet, and the spread is 2½–3 feet. Its appearance is irregular and semi-arching.

CUPRESSUS Lawsoniana Ellwoodii. Lovely blue-grey foliage and a good plant for the rockery. It is oval and dense in appearance.

o **C. L. Fletcherii.** Bluish-grey feathery foliage. When planted the height is 1–3 feet, but its ultimate height and spread are 8–15 feet, and 4–6 feet respectively. It has a bushy and upright habit, and likes ordinary well-drained soil.

C. L. Forsteckiana. Has a distinctive appearance, green foliage arranged in whorls. The height and spread are : 2–2½ feet, and 3–3½ feet. Its habit is spreading and rather spraying, and broadly rounded with age. Ordinary well-drained soil is best.

C. obtusa nana. A beautiful dwarf conifer with bright green leaves arranged in close whorls. It has a low, spreading and pyramidal shape, and likes ordinary well-drained soil on the moist side.

o **C. pisifera ericoides.** The foliage goes bronzy-red in the winter. Its height when bought is 1½–2½ feet, but eventually it is 6–9 feet tall and spreads 3–5 feet. The appearance is broadly pyramidal. The soil should be ordinary and slightly moist.

o **C. p. filifolia.** Arching thread-like foliage. Slow growing. When planted is 1½–2 feet tall, but it eventually is 5–7 feet in height and covers 8–9 feet. The habit is arching and spreading.

C. p. nana aurea variegata. Very dwarf, slow growing variety whose branchlets are tipped with gold. Is low and cushion-like in habit. Well drained, slightly moist soil.

C. p. plumosa aurea compacta. A pretty variety with broken golden sprays of rather feathery foliage. Height 4–5 inches, spread 12–15 inches. Is low, flat-topped and spreading in habit. Ordinary well-drained soil, slightly moist.

JUNIPERUS communis prostrata. Very low growing, with grey-green foliage. While its height is only 4–6 inches, the spread is indefinite. The habit is prostrate and creeping. Grows best in moist, but well-drained soil.

J. c. compressa. A very choice dwarf conifer. A dense pyramid of fine bluish-grey foliage, and column-like in habit. It is only 5–6 inches tall when planted, but seldom exceeds 2 feet. Ordinary well-drained, slightly moist soil.

o **J. Sabina tamariscifolia.** Low-growing and of spreading habit. The maximum height is 3 feet, and the spread is 5–7 feet. Is prostrate in flat tiers in appearance. Ordinary well-drained soil, damp.

PICEA Albertiana conica. A perfectly cone-shaped variety with bright green foliage densely packed. Height is 4½–6 feet, and the spread is 2–3 feet. Ordinary soil, well-drained but on the moist side.

P. excelsa Remontii. Very slow growing variety. The leaves are a soft yellowish-green. Height is 2½–3½ feet, and the spread is 2–3 feet. It looks broadly conical, and likes ordinary well-drained soil.

THUYA Lobbii Ellwangeriana Rheingold. A beautiful variety with gold foliage in the summer, turning bronzy-red in the winter. When planted may be 12–18 inches tall, but is eventually 3–5 feet, and a spread of 4–6 feet. It is globose or broadly pyramidal in appearance and likes ordinary damp soil.

T. occidentalis compacta. A globular ball of bright green foliage. A fairly strong grower and has an eventual diameter of 5 feet. Its height is 4–5 feet, and it spreads 4–5 feet. Ordinary well-drained soil.

T. o. globosa (Little Gem). A miniature of the above with finer foliage. Height 2–2½ feet, and spread 2–2½ feet. Ordinary well-drained soil.

HARDY FERNS

Hardy ferns give an added interest to the rock garden. They are moderate in their requirements, most of them prefer shade and a uniformly cool position all through the year.

They can, however, grow in many different situations, some like to be in an exposed place where they can receive the splashings from the stream as it tumbles down. Some like to grow upside down in any natural-looking baby cavern which can be produced. Some of them prefer a fairly moist soil, while others seem to grow quite happily in dry spots wedged in between two large pieces of stone.

After all, one can have too much colour in the rock garden. If you have nothing but a blaze of blossom, the whole effect is apt to be a bit dazzling, and so it is useful to be able to have some foliage plants to act as a background or as a foil. Nature, herself, goes in for green tremendously ; she invariably has her flowers against a green background, and when planning our rock garden we must remember this. As in the case of shrubs, there are evergreen ferns and also those which lose their foliage in the winter months. Many a bare rock can be furnished with an evergreen fern which cheers it up no end.

Only use sufficient ferns in your rock garden so as to provide what green background is necessary. Don't overdo it, whatever you do. If you particularly like ferns, because you enjoy the coolness or the elegance of the foliage, there is no reason why more should not be planted than usual, but generally speaking, the ferns will grow in a cool, shady spot and by the banks of any little stream which may be provided, so that moisture is never scarce.

The soil mixture used for ferns is usually really well decayed leaf mould which is black and spongy, plus the addition of some silver sand to keep it open. No attempt should be made to firm this material hard when it is placed into the " pocket " where the ferns are to go. Just get out a little hole, put in the roots, and then, if possible, place a small stone over the roots before the leaves are pressed back into position. Some gardeners like to mix a little fine broken slate—slate chippings as they are called—in with the black leaf mould just to keep it " in condition " as they term it.

The planting of the deciduous species (those that lose their leaves in the winter) may be done from the middle of March to the middle of April. The evergreen species are often planted at the same time but can be put in, if preferred, from mid-August to mid-September.

I want to make it quite clear, that personally I don't think a fern is terribly important in a rock garden, as compared with the many other plants that are available. I have, therefore, only included a few species in the list which will be found on page 57, and those who are particularly interested in ferns of all kinds, may study some authoritative work on this subject.

A LIST OF SHRUBS SUITABLE FOR THE ROCKERY

Name	Description	Height	Season	Remarks
Andromeda polifolia	Grey leaves, white, urn-like flowers, twiggy shrub	1'–2'	April–August	Peaty soil, semi-shade
Azalea Hinodegiri	Bright crimson flowers. Evergreen	2'–3'	April–May	Sandy, peaty soil, semi-shade
Berberis buxifolia nana	Orange yellow flowers, purple fruit. Dwarf compact evergreen	2'	April–May	Most soils, sunny spot
B. concinna	Leaves, green above and white below. Vivid in the autumn. Orange flowers and red berries.	1'–3'	April–May	Most soils, sunny spot
B. Darwinnii	Dark green leaves, orange yellow flowers. Evergreen	6'–12'	April	Most soils, sunny spot
Cassiope tetragona	Tiny, bell-like flowers, pink, hanging from shoots on thread-like stems	6"–12"	March–June	Moist, sandy, peat
Cistus crispus	Deep rose flowers 2 inches across. Evergreen	2'	June	Dry, sandy, limey soil Full sun
C. purpureus	Purple flowers, marked in dark red	3'–4'	June	See above
C. salvifolius	White flowers	2'	June–July	See above
C. Silver Pink	Pink flowers	3'–4'	June–July	See above
Cotoneaster congesta	Pinkish flowers, vivid red fruit. Brilliant autumnal foliage. Evergreen	6'	April–May	Moist soil, chalky
C. horizontalis	Semi-evergreen. Pink flowers, red fruit	3'	April–May	Moist soil, chalky
C. microphylla	Arching branches with white flowers, red berries	4'	April–May	Moist soil, chalky
Cytisus Ardoinii (Broom)	Golden yellow flowers	1'–2'	April–May	Light, well drained, sun or partial shade
C. kewensis	Cream flowers	6"–12"	May–June	See above
C. praecox	Light yellow flowers	3'–4'	April–May	See above

Name	Description	Height	Season	Remarks
Daphne blagayana	Creamy white, scented flowers, evergreen, spreading habit	9″–12″	March–April	Well drained, slightly acid soil or stony soil
D. Cneorum	Fragrant, pink flowers. Evergreen. Trailing habit	10″–12″	April–May	See above
Erica carnea	White, pink or crimson flowers	6″–9″	Dec.–May	Sandy, peaty soil, sun or semi-shade. Likes lime
E. cinerea	White, pink or crimson flowers	6″–9″	July–Sept.	Dislikes lime
E. mediterranea	Scented pink flowers	4″–10″	March–May	Dislikes lime
Euonymus radicans	Dark green foliage, flowers inconspicuous	1′–2′	July–Sept.	Semi-shade, or under trees
Fuchsia procumbens	Brown and yellow flowers, large, pink berries	3″–4″	June–October	Sheltered sunny spot
F. pumila	Red and purple flowers	12″–18″	June–October	See above
F. Riccartonii	Red and purple flowers	4′–5′	June–October	See above
F. Tom Thumb	Red and purple flowers	8″–12″	June–July	See above
Gaultheria	Pinkish white flowers and bright red berries	6″–9″	July–August	Peaty, limeless soil, some shade
Genista dalmatica	Rare species, like a dwarf gorse bush, gold flowers	¾′–2′	June–July	Light, well drained soil, sunny
G. Hispanica	Bright green leaves and bright yellow flowers	1′–1½′	May–June	See above
G. pilosa	Prostrate habit. Bright yellow flowers	12″–18″	June–July	See above
G. sagittalis	Golden flowers	6″–12″	May–Sept.	See above
G. tinctoria flore pleno	Double golden flowers	1′–2′	July–August	See above
Hedera Helix minima	Yellowish green foliage	6′–8′		Most soils, any position
Potentilla fruticosa	Silvery leaves, large, white flowers	2′–3′	May–August	Deep, sandy soil, sunny spot
Rhododendron ferrugineum (Alpenrose)	Many tubular rose pink flowers	1′–2′	April–June	Will grow in limey soil
R. racemosum	White and rose pink flowers	2′–3′	April–May	Dislikes lime in soil
Spiraea bullata	Scarlet rose flowers	2′–3′	July–August	Moist loam, some shade

S. Antony Waterer	Crimson flowers	2'–3'		
Veronica carnosula	Evergreen, greyish leaves and white flowers	1'–2'	June–October	Moist loam, some shade
V. cupressoides	Similar to conifer in appearance, white flowers tinted with lavender	½'–3'	Summer	
V. Hectori (Whipcord Veronica)	Lilac flowers	1'–2'	June–July	
V. pimeleoides	Glaucous, blue grey leaves, purple	½'–1'	June–July	

A LIST OF FERNS SUITABLE FOR THE WATER GARDEN AND ROCKERY

Name	Description	Height	Remarks
Adiantum Capillus-Veneris (Hardy Maidenhair)	Green leaves	6"	Likes moist, shady place, with loam, sand, and leaf mould
A. pedatum (Maidenhair fern)	Delicate green leaves	1'–3'	Plant in a sheltered spot, free from frost. Moist, leafy soil, partial shade
Allosorus crispa (Parsley Fern)	Foliage like Parsley	3"–6"	Drained, shady soil of loam, leaf mould, sandstone
Asplenium Adiantum nigrum (Black Spleenwort)	Shining dark green leaves, similar to Maidenhair fern	6"–18"	Likes a shady cool spot, and will grow in damp or fairly dry soil. Evergreen foliage
A. rutamuraria (Wall Rue)	Small green fronds like Maidenhair fern	3"–6"	See above
A. trichomanes (Maidenhair Spleenwort)	Delicate and wiry fronds	3"–6"	See above
Blechnum penna marina	Fronds are almost erect, evergreen, dark olive-green	4"–6"	Cool, moist position by water. Full sun or semi-shade
Ceterach officinarum (Scaly Spleenwort)	Evergreen rosettes of olive-green leaves with brown undersides	6"	Dry, shady soil. Some mortar-rubble helpful. Evergreen foliage
Cysopteris fragilis	Pale green fronds	6"	Dry, shady soil, some mortar-rubble

Name	Description	Height	Remarks
Onoclea sensibilis (Sensitive Fern)	Arching fronds like oak leaves, pale green	1'–1½'	Likes very damp soil, and will even grow in shallow water. Sun or semi-shade
Osmunda cinnamonea (Cinnamon Fern)	Rich green fronds, young stems are covered with rusty down	3'–5'	Will grow in sun or shade, but roots must be near water
O. regalis (Royal Fern)	Pale green fronds, going rusty in the autumn	4'–5'	Roots should be close to the water
Phyllitis Scolopendrium (Hart's Tongue)	Shining, bright green fronds	1'–2'	Will grow in wet or moist, shady positions
Polypodium Dryopteris (Oak Fern)	Crinkled, evergreen fronds	4"	Moist, shady soil
P. vulgare cambricum	Broad, feathery fronds. Olive-green to russet-brown in colour	2'	Will grow in wet or moist, shady positions
Polystichum Lonchitis	Green fronds	6"	Sun. Loam, leaf, peat, sand
Woodsia ilvensis	Hoary-looking	6"	Cool, dry, shaded soil

CHAPTER IX

BULMS

Real babies I love—do I ? Yes.
1. The " babies " are just right in the rock garden.
2. How deep shall I plant them ?
3. They need so little attention.
4. What kinds shall I choose ?
5. When ?

ORDINARY daffodils and tulips, of course, look out of place in the rock garden, being tall and " gross " in comparison with their smaller growing miniature neighbours. There are, however, a number of baby bulbous and tuberous rooted plants which can be grown, since they add interest as well as colour to this garden. Many of them come from mountainous districts of Europe and Asia, the Pyrenees seems to specialize in the " babies " of the narcissus species. As they have what may be called an Alpine background and birthright, they certainly deserve a place in our rock garden.

Planting should be done in late summer or early autumn. The autumn and winter flowering plants must be in, of course, by August, but September or October is quite soon enough for planting those which bloom in the spring. The taller growing kinds such as the Alliums, Anemones, Fritillarias, Sternbergias and Tulip species should be planted from three to six inches deep, depending on the size of the bulb (the smaller the shallower), and four to eight inches apart (the dwarfer the closer they go). The remainder of the bulbs found in the list which follows may be planted from one and a half to four inches deep, and from one inch to three inches apart, according to the size of the bulb.

On the whole, most of the plants enjoy an open situation with all the sun they can get, and will thrive in ordinary soil. Exceptions are the Colchicums and Sternbergias which require a fairly deep, rich soil ; the Anemones which seem to like a rich and moist soil, and the Trilliums which prefer partial shade and a moist, peaty soil.

When once established, the majority can be left down for a number of years. Little attention is needed beyond keeping down weeds and clearing away the withered foliage at the end of the growing season. The Tulips, perhaps, will benefit by being lifted and rested each year, or at least every two years, and also the Irises, in all but the warmest districts.

LIST OF BULBS FOR THE ROCK GARDEN
with brief descriptions
See also pages 78 to 125.

ALLIUM. Miniature onion-like plants with narrow leaves, and heads of small flowers.

> **A. cæruleum (azureum).** Deep blue flowers. 18 inches, July.
>
> **A. Moly luteum.** Bright yellow flowers. 12 inches, June to July.
>
> **A. Ostrowskianum.** Reddish violet flowers. 12 inches, June to July.

ANEMONE. The brightly coloured large-flowered kinds are well known. Those species suitable for the rock garden are similar, but daintier and altogether smaller.

> **A. apennina.** Lavender-blue daisy-like flowers in March. 6 inches tall.
>
> **A. blanda.** Blue flowers. There is also a pink variety. 6 inches, January–March. Requires rather a sheltered position.
>
> **A. fulgens.** Vivid scarlet flowers with a black centre. There is also a double variety. 12 inches, May. Requires a partially shaded position.
>
> **A. nemerosa Allenii.** Lavender-purple flowers in January–March. 6 inches.
>
> **A. ranunculoides.** Clear golden-yellow flowers. 6–12 inches, March.

BRODIAEA GRANDIFLORA. Bright blue clusters of flowers in June. 6 inches.

BULBOCODIUM VERNUM. (Meadow Saffron). Violet flowers in January. 4–6 inches. Very free-flowering.

CHIONODOXA. Dwarf plants with small hyacinth-like leaves, and 2 or 3 flowers per stem.

> **C. Luciliae.** Bright blue flowers with white centres. There is also a white and pink variety. 4–6 inches, March.
> **C. Luciliae rosea.** Rose flowers in March. 6 inches.
> **C. Sardensis.** Gentian blue flowers with a white centre. 4–6 inches, March.

COLCHICUM. Plants with crocus-like flowers but wider leaves, similar to those of a daffodil.

> **C. autumnale.** Purplish-pink flowers. 6–8 inches, September–October.
> **C. speciosum.** Rosy-purple flowers. September.

CONVALLARIA MAJALIS. (Lily of the Valley). White scented flowers in May. 1 foot.

CROCUS. The smaller-flowered species are more suitable for the rock garden than the larger-flowered, garden varieties.

> **C. biflorus.** Purple flowers stained with buff on the outside and delicate lavender inside.
> **C. Imperati.** Inner petals violet, outer petals fawn. 6 inches, January–March. The earliest crocus to flower.
> **C. pulchellus.** Lavender with paler veins and a golden throat. 6 inches, Autumn.
> **C. sativus.** Purplish-lilac, feathered with violet. The stigma is long and blood red in colour. 6 inches, Autumn.
> **C. Sieberi.** Soft lavender-blue with orange throat and stigma. 6 inches, February–March.

C. **speciosus.** Violet-blue flowers, veined with deeper violet and orange-red stigma. The variety **Aitchisoni** is light blue.

C. **Tomasinianus.** Pale blue flowers. 3 inches, March.

C. **versicolor.** White flowers, faintly striped with purple and a yellow throat. 6 inches, March.

C. **zonatus.** Rosy-lilac. 6 inches, Autumn.

CYCLAMEN. Dwarf species are all hardy. Autumn flowering kinds should be planted between January and July. Spring flowering kinds from July to September.

C. **africanum.** Bluish-lilac flowers with a purplish centre. 4-6 inches, Autumn.

C. **Atkinsii.** Flowers vary from white to crimson. 4 inches, February–March.

C. **cilicicum.** White and purple flowers. 6 inches, January.

C. **Coum.** Deep rosy-red. 4 inches, February–March.

C. **europaeum.** Crimson, sweetly scented flowers and silvery marked leaves. 4 inches, August.

C. **ibericum.** Similar to C. Coum but the leaves are marked with silver. 3-4 inches, February–March.

C. **neapolitanum.** Rose-pink flowers and ivy-like leaves marbled with silver. 4 inches, Autumn. The flowers are out before the leaves appear.

C. **repandum.** Bright crimson flowers with silver marbled foliage. 4 inches, March and May.

ERANTHIS. This cheery little plant is well known. The flowers are bright yellow, similar to, and about the same size as, those of a buttercup. There is a green frill just below each flower.

E. **cilicica.** Slightly larger flowers. 3 inches, Spring.

E. **hyemalis.** Long-stalked leaves. 3 inches, January–March.

ERYTHRONIUM. These are small plants with flowers shaped something like those of a cyclamen.

E. americanum. Yellow flowers, spotted red. 6 inches, April–May.

E. Dens-canis. Rose-pink flowers. There are also white and purple varieties. 3–6 inches, April–May.

E. grandiflorum. Yellow flowers. 6–9 inches, April–May.

E. Hartwegi. Creamy-white flowers. 6 inches, May.

FRITILLARIA. These plants have drooping bell-shaped flowers, beautifully marked with fine lines.

F. citrina. Pale yellow flowers. 8–12 inches, May.

F. Meleagris. Purple and cream-coloured flowers. 12 inches, April and May. This species grows wild in Britain.

F. pudica. Bright yellow flowers. 4–6 inches, April–May.

GALANTHUS. These bulbs are extremely useful because they are so early flowering.

G. byzantinus. The large white flowers are marked with green. 8 inches, January.

G. Elwesii. The large white flowers are marked with green. 8 inches, January.

G. plicatus. Large white flowers. Very vigorous. 9 inches, February.

IRIS. The best known kinds suitable for the rock garden are some of the dwarf bulbous sorts. On the whole, they are early flowering.

I. alata. The flowers vary from lavender-blue to deep lavender, with a golden keel. 6–12 inches, January.

I. Danfordiae. Yellow and brown flowers. 3 inches, February.

I. histroides major. Blue, yellow and violet. 6 inches, February.

I. reticulata. Sweetly-scented, deep violet-purple flowers, with yellow markings. 6–12 inches, February.

IXIA. These are taller than the majority of the plants, but they are attractive and graceful, several flowers being produced on a wiry stem. There are many varieties, varying in colour from white with red or dark purple centres to yellow, orange, pink or red. Some are double. 12–21 inches, May–July.

LEUCOJUM AUTUMNALE. White and pink flowers. 4 inches, October.

MUSCARI. Small plants with bluebell-like leaves and heads of small flowers tightly packed together, not unlike a bunch of grapes.

> **M. armeniacum.** Violet flowers. 6 inches, May.
>
> **M. botryoides.** Pure white flowers. There is also a dark blue variety. 6 inches, March.
>
> **M. moschatum.** Greyish-purple flowers. 6 inches, March.
>
> **M. paradoxum.** Bluish-black flowers. The darkest of all. 6–7 inches. March and April.
>
> **M. plumosum.** The spike of violet flowers has a feathery appearance. 6 inches, April.
>
> **M. racemosum.** Very deep blue flowers. 6 inches, April.

NARCISSUS. There are a number of " baby " daffodils, all quite hardy.

> **N. bulbocodium.** The leaves are narrow and the rich yellow flowers have a cone-shaped trumpet. 6 inches, April. Prefers a moist situation. There are also pale yellow and white varieties.
>
> **N. cyclamineus.** Rich yellow flowers ; the petals are reflexed, making the flowers similar in appearance to a cyclamen flower. The leaves are narrow and rush-like. 6 inches, February and March. Prefers a moist situation.
>
> **N. minimus.** The smallest of all trumpet daffodils.

Tulipa
dasystemon
makes a
charming pot
plant for the
alpine house.

Androsace
yunnanense
spreads rapidly,
but is welcome
for its cheerful
rosy flowers so
freely produced.

The flowers are a citron-yellow colour. 3 inches, February.

N. minor. Another small trumpet daffodil, golden-yellow in colour. 6 inches, March.

N. moschatus. White, with pale citron-coloured cup. 12 inches, April.

N. triandrus albus. A small creamy-white narcissus with reflexed petals. The variety **calathinus** has larger flowers. 6–7 inches, March.

ORNITHOGALUM ARABICUM. Fragrant, star-like white flowers, with black centres. 18 inches, June.

SCILLA. Dwarf plants with bluebell-like leaves and bell-shaped flowers, one or two per stem. Enjoys partial shade.

S. bifolia. Deep blue flowers. 3–6 inches, March.

S. sibirica. Bright blue flowers. 3–6 inches, February.

S. s. alba. White flowers. 3–6 inches, February.

STERNBERGIA COLCHICIFLORA. Yellow flowers. 4 inches, September.

S. lutea major. Effective crocus-like flowers of a rich golden-yellow colour. 12 inches, September.

TULIPA. Several of the tulip species are suitable for the rock garden. They are smaller-flowered and more graceful than the ordinary garden varieties.

T. biflora. Creamy-yellow flowers. 8 inches, May.

T. Greigii. The flowers are a glowing vermilion-scarlet tinted with orange. The leaves are spotted. 9–13 inches, May.

T. Kaufmanniana. The petals are creamy-white, with a golden base inside, and a dull, strawberry-red broad stripe outside. There are many beautiful named varieties. 6–8 inches, May.

T. K. aurea. White and carmine flowers with yellow margin. 9 inches, May.

T. praestans. Large flowers of vivid scarlet, borne two to three on a stem. 12 inches, April.

T. pulchella. Rosy-mauve flowers. 6 inches, May.

C

CHAPTER X

GENERAL MANAGEMENT AND PROPAGATION

What to do !—
1. In Spring.
2. Keep down the weeds.
3. At Autumn time.
4. Be clean.
5. Raise plants !

ROUTINE CULTIVATION. The routine cultivation of the rock garden may be divided into three definite periods, (a) Spring, (b) Summer, (c) Autumn.

SPRING. The whole of the garden may be given a light top dressing with a compost consisting of one part good soil (sterilized if possible), one part silver sand, and one-quarter part horticultural peat or rotted leaves. The whole should be rubbed through a $\frac{1}{4}$ inch sieve. It is necessary to work some of this compost in among the tops of the mossy Saxifrages, but this can only be done on a dry day and when the plants are in a dry condition. The compost must be really dry also. The rosettes may be packed tightly in this material. If, however, there is any moisture about, they will rot off.

Any rocks that have been loosened by frost during the winter should be made firm. The soil in the pockets that has been loosened should be packed down firmly, and any soil that has obviously been washed away should be replaced. See if any of the plants on the steeper slopes have been washed away, and replace them. Should the weather be dry, copious watering will be necessary ; in an attempt to hold in the moisture, place small pieces of stone around the choicer plants.

Everything should be done to keep down weeds and so prevent seeding. This means a fair amount of hand-weeding, an operation which is not as tedious in the rock garden as it is in the flat formal bed. A three-pronged carving fork will be found useful for disturbing the weeds and for breaking up the ground. A hoe should never be used in a rock garden, for it destroys the Alpine seedlings which are so often worth keeping.

A look-out should be kept for slugs and other pests at this time, and a determined effort to control them early in the year will save a lot of disappointment later.

USEFUL TOOLS FOR THE ROCK GARDEN

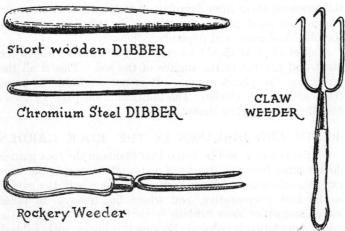

Short wooden DIBBER

Chromium Steel DIBBER

CLAW WEEDER

Rockery Weeder

SUMMER. Keep on weeding and hand forking all through the summer, though if the weeding has been thorough in the spring, there is not much of this work later. The surface of the soil should, however, be stirred with the hand fork from time to time. If the summer is hot it may be necessary to give thorough waterings occasionally, and after each soaking the soil should be loosened again, so as to keep a surface mulch. As each plant ceases to flower, the flowering heads should be removed, unless they are being left on for seed-saving purposes. The straggly plants should certainly be cut back after flowering, and it is often necessary to cut them back quite hard. Certain of the older plants may need dividing, cuttings may be taken from some plants, and seeds saved from others.

AUTUMN. This is the time for a certain amount of renovation. Some old pockets of hardier plants will need disturbing, because the soil is exhausted, and they can then be cleared out, re-made, and re-planted. The dead growth should be cut back, and any leaves from trees that fall on to the rock garden should be removed immediately. The woolly-leaved plants should be protected by sheets of glass ; this prevents them from damping off from excessive moisture. Plants that need particular attention in this connection are Raoulia, Androsace and Asperula.

A sheet of glass should be erected 5 or 6 inches above the plant and parallel to the surface of the soil. This is all the protection the plants require. It is not advisable to cover them with a tent cloche. The illustration on page 23 shows how the sheet of glass should be used.

PESTS AND DISEASES IN THE ROCK GARDEN

On the whole, it will be found that plants in the rock garden do not suffer from the attacks of pests and diseases to the same extent as do vegetables and fruits. Cleanliness in the garden is the best preventative, and where the removal of fallen leaves and other loose rubbish is carried out thoroughly, the insect population is reduced, because it is under such rubbish that many insects lie hidden all the winter.

SLUGS AND SNAILS. These can be very troublesome in spring, eating off the tender young shoots as they start to grow.

Control. The best scheme is to poison them, by putting down a bait containing Metaldehyde. The bait can be bought ready mixed, or can be mixed at home, using one metaldehyde bar crushed to a powder, and mixed with a " carrier " such as bread crumbs, dried tea leaves or bone meal ; bran is the perfect carrier when obtainable. The bait should be put in little piles about the garden—a dessertspoonful at a time is ample—and by the next morning, many poisoned slugs and snails will be found, these are best cleared away as they are very unsightly.

Warning. Metaldehyde is poisonous to humans also, so keep the tin clearly marked, and out of the reach of children.

WOODLICE. These are a nuisance, nibbling through stems at ground level and feeding on young roots.

Control. D.D.T. powder sprinkled about the ground near large stones or by cracks where the woodlice congregate will soon remove these pests.

WIREWORM. These are sometimes introduced in new loam. Examine the loam carefully when preparing it, and remove all the insects which are found. Trapping with pieces of carrot stuck in the ground, should remove those missed at first. The carrot attracts the wireworm, examine the pieces each morning, and remove and kill any insects found in them.

APHIS. The usual collection of Greenfly, Blackfly and other " colours " of this all too well-known pest will attack rock plants at all stages.

Control. The secret of successful control is to start early —a day's delay after the first fly is seen, allows time for literally hundreds more to be hatched out. Spray with insecticides containing nicotine or derris, and give additional sprayings at intervals afterwards, to kill off any " stragglers". Alternatively, a dust containing the same substances can be used, and would be better for the plants that do not like damp.

EELWORM. This minute pest is invisible to the naked eye, but its effect will be recognised in the rock garden, where it often attacks Cheiranthus. The new growths look very " bunchy " like the Robins-pin-cushions seen on wild roses.

Control. The only practical control in the ordinary small garden, is to pull up and burn all infected plants, and only take cuttings from those that show no sign of the complaint.

DISEASES

MILDEW is the only disease that is likely to cause damage in the rock garden, and that only in dull, damp weather.

Control. Prevention is the best cure in this case. A healthy plant, growing in a suitable position will seldom suffer, and attention to good drainage is the first step in the battle against the disease. Dusting with Flowers of Sulphur will help to prevent the spread of the disease, if an attack does start.

DAMPING OFF. This is a disease that can cause a lot of damage in the early stages, when raising seedlings.

Control. Water all seed pans and boxes of pricked-off seedlings with Cheshunt Compound. This can be bought ready mixed in tins, and only needs to be diluted according to the instructions. Wash all the cans carefully after use, as the compound contains copper sulphate, which corrodes metal watering cans.

PROPAGATION

Rock plants may be propagated in four ways : by seeds, division, cuttings and layers. Anyone keen on a rock garden is advised to take some interest in the raising of new plants, for the life of the average Alpine is about 5 years. A brick frame, facing north, is perhaps the ideal place for the raising of the young rock plants. A well-built brick or concrete frame keeps cool and, facing north, does not dry out so quickly. The young plants can be placed here, in their pots plunged up to their rims in ashes. The lights need only to be put into position if the weather is very wet, and even then, wooden blocks can be put underneath, so as to lift them up to allow free ventilation. During frosty weather, the lights may be closed if the plants have been watered recently.

SEEDS. Raising plants from seeds does ensure that they will be healthy and vigorous. It is a good method of acclimatizing imported strains, and of course, of raising new varieties. The seeds should be gathered just as they become

COLD FRAME for Propagation
(Sloping to the North)

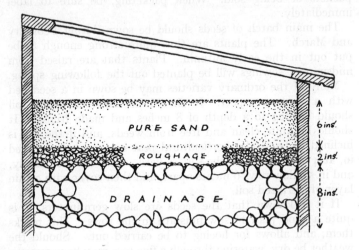

PURE SAND — 6 ins.

ROUGHAGE — 2 ins.

DRAINAGE — 8 ins.

WATERING SEEDLINGS

ripe and are ready to fall (they should never be gathered green). They should then be placed in a shallow receptacle and baked in the sun for a week or so, before being put into packets or being sold. When packeting, be sure to label immediately.

The main batch of seeds should be sown during February and March. The plants are thus quite strong enough to be put out in the early autumn. Plants that are raised from midsummer sowings will be planted out the following spring.

Many of the ordinary varieties may be sown in a seed bed with a western aspect. It should be sheltered. The soil should be dug to a depth of 8 inches and made friable. It should be quite clean and free from weeds, and if the soil is inclined to be sandy, horticultural peat moss may be worked in, at 4 or 5 ounces to the square yard. Sow the seed thinly, and in shallow rows 6 inches apart, and then cover with a thin layer of sterilized soil.

If it is known that the seeds are slow germinators, it is quite a good plan to sow mustard in the rows. This marks them, and allows for hoeing to be carried out. Should the weather be dry, watering through a fine rose may be necessary, and if slugs are a nuisance, put down metaldehyde bait. Where only a few seeds are to be sown, or where the variety is rare, it is worth while sowing in pans or pots. These should be crocked to about a third of their depth, the crocks covered with sphagnum moss and the pans filled up with a compost consisting of two parts of good soil, one part of well-rotted leaf, passed through a $\frac{1}{4}$ inch sieve, and one part coarse silver sand. This compost should be sterilized before use. It is possible to do this by pouring boiling water over the soil, and then waiting two days before sowing the seed. The seeds should be mixed with three times the quantity of sand, and then sown thinly. A little of the sterilized compost should then be sifted over the top from a fine-meshed sieve.

A sheet of glass should be put over each pan, and this should be removed each day and wiped dry to remove the condensation. Watering should be done by plunging the pans

WHERE TO LOOK FOR ROOTS

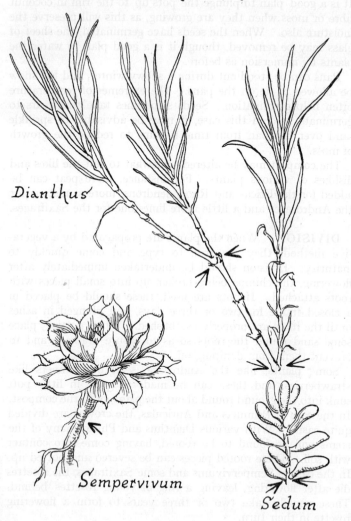

up to the rim in a bucket of tepid water for a minute or so. It is a good plan to plunge the pots up to the rim in coconut fibre or moss when they are growing, as this will preserve the moisture also. When the seeds have germinated, the sheet of glass may be removed, though it is a good plan to water the plants by immersion as before.

Pans can be stood out during a snowy winter, and the snow be allowed to lie on the pans. The extremes of temperature often help germination. Seeds sometimes take two years to germinate, and in this case, it may be advisable to sprinkle sand over the pan from time to time to reduce the growth of moss.

The compost may be altered somewhat to suit the likes and dislikes of various plants. For instance, more peat can be added for the Ericas and Rhododendrons, more sandstone for the Androsaces and a little more limestone for the Saxifrages.

DIVISION. When the plants are propagated by a vegetative method, they are true to type and come quickly to maturity. Division should be undertaken immediately after flowering, the clumps being broken up into small pieces with roots attached. If pots are used, these should be placed in a closed frame for two or three days, and plunged in ashes until the roots are properly established. When potting, place some sand round the roots so as to ensure drainage and to prevent them from damping off.

Some plants, like the Androsace, send out runners like strawberries, and these can be made to grow in little pots sunk into the ground round about the plant, or in the compost. In the case of Primulas and Auriculas, the crowns are divided quite easily. With various Dianthus and Phlox, many of the stems will be found to be rooted, having come into contact with soil. These rooted pieces can be severed and potted up. In the case of Sempervivums and some Saxifrages, the rosettes die after flowering, leaving a ring of young rosettes behind. These usually take two or three years to form a flowering rosette in their turn.

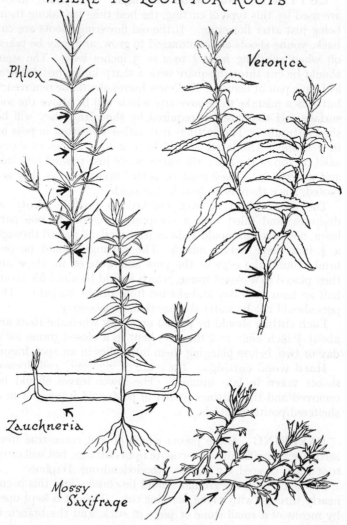

WHERE TO LOOK FOR ROOTS

Phlox

Veronica

Zauchneria

Mossy
Saxifrage

CUTTINGS. Soft wood cuttings. New young shoots are used for this type of cutting, the best time for taking them being just after flowering. If the old flowering shoots are cut back, young shoots are encouraged to grow, and may be taken off when anything from ½ to 2 or 3 inches long. The stem should be cut through square with a sharp knife, just below a leaf, or a pair of leaves. The lower leaves should be removed,* but it is a mistake to remove any which will be above the soil surface. If they are not required by the plant, they will be shed naturally. The cuttings may either be rooted in pots or in a frame. The latter should have 2 to 4 inches of damp sand on top of the soil ; the cuttings are just pushed into this and watered in. They must be potted up as soon as they are rooted, since there is no food in the sand.

The pots should be well crocked to provide plenty of drainage, and filled with a compost consisting of one part loam, one part leaf mould and one part sand, all passed through a ¼ inch sieve before mixing. The cuttings should be put firmly round the edge of the pots and watered in, these are then placed in a closed frame, which should be aired for about half an hour each day and shaded from bright sunlight. The pots should not be watered more than is necessary.

Each cutting should be potted up singly when the roots are about ½ inch long, and the pots kept in a closed frame for a day or two, before plunging them into ashes in an open frame.

Hard wood cuttings. These are of vigorous, well-ripened shoots taken in late summer. The lower leaves should be removed and the cuttings rooted in pots, cold frames, or in a sheltered position outside.

LAYERING. Some plants which do not come true from seed, are also difficult to propagate from cuttings, but will often root when layered, e.g. Ericas, Rhododendrons, Daphne.

A branch near the ground should be chosen, and this is cut nearly through with a long, slanting cut. The cut is kept open by means of a small stone or piece of stick, and the branch is

* As this book goes to press—(I understand that the latest practice at Edinburgh Botanic Gardens is to leave the leaves on.)

pegged down firmly into a heap of sandy compost. The end of the branch should be tied to a stake, to prevent it from being blown out of the ground before it has rooted. If the branches are too high up to reach the ground, the best plan is to break a pot longitudinally in half and tie it, full of compost, round the cut branch, but watering will need to be done very frequently in hot weather.

Layering is usually done in autumn, and the branches are examined the following spring. If they have rooted, the branch is severed between the parent plant and the newly-formed roots, and the layer may be moved a month or two later. It is important to keep the soil moist from the time of layering until the new plant is well rooted.

All pot Alpines are best kept plunged in ashes; in this way the soil is kept from drying out, the temperature remains fairly even, and the pots are not so liable to crack in frosty weather.

CHAPTER XI

LISTS OF ROCK PLANTS WITH DIRECTIONS AND INSTRUCTIONS

I think this chapter is about plants !
1. What are the best plants ?
2. Which plants are which ?
3. More about plants.
4. Yet more plants.
5. Many different plants.

ACAENA. New Zealand Burr. Low-growing carpeting plants with inconspicuous flowers and attractive foliage in various shades. Very suitable for paving and steps as they stand up to a certain amount of traffic. They grow in practically any soil and manage to thrive in sun or shade. Do not plant them near any of the weak growing treasures because they quickly cover a large area. Increased by division.

A. Buchanani. Pale silvery green leaves. Inconspicuous flowers in July and August, 2 inches.

A. microphylla. Very decorative bronze leaves. The seed heads are colourful, being covered with bright red spines. July and August, 3 inches.

A. m. inermis. Bronze leaves slightly larger than the preceding. The dull little flower heads are borne on 4-inch stems.

ACANTHOLIMON. Prickly Thrift. The plant forms a mound of spiney leaves just like a grey green hedgehog, covered in June with sprays of flowers. They need a position in full sun and require a very well drained soil. Propagation is difficult and only a small proportion of the cuttings taken will form roots, but these should be taken in summer and put in a sand frame.

A. glumaceum. Flowers light rose in June, 6 inches.

A. venustum. Rose pink on an arched spike 6 inches high. A difficult plant.

78

ACHILLEA. Milfoil. Many of these are common wayside herbs, and all have aromatic foliage. Useful for the mat of grey or green leaves which make a good winter carpet, as well as producing a mass of flowers in early summer. Will grow in any light, well drained soil in full sun. Increase by division which can be done successfully directly after flowering when the dead heads are being removed, this gives the plants time to form neat tufts before winter sets in.

  A. argentea. Silvery leaf. Clusters of white daisy flowers in June, 6 inches.

  A. Lewisii. (Syn. King Edward). Grey green leaves. Flowers a delicate sulphur yellow, these appear in succession from May till September. 9 inches. Definitely the most useful owing to its long flowering season, and colour which blends so well with other flowers. Not so rampant as the others, and needs to be lifted fairly frequently and the young pieces replanted in good soil, otherwise it tends to exhaust itself by over blooming, leaving the young shoots very weak.

  A. rupestris. Smooth green leaves. Heads of white flowers in June, 6 inches.

  A. tomentosa. Green ferny leaves. Flowers bright mustard yellow in July, 9 inches.

  A. umbellata. A mat of silvery leaves. White flowers in June, 6 inches.

AETHIONEMA. The ones grown in rock gardens are mostly miniature bushlets and deserve a place in every collection. They need full sun and do best in a light, well drained loam which contains some lime. Can be easily raised from seed which gives the healthiest plants, though the named hybrids have to be increased by cuttings of the young shoots which appear after flowering. Keep the plants cut back after flowering and they will remain neat bushes for many years.

  A. armenum. Neat little wiry bushlet with grey green leaves. Long spikes of pale pink flowers in May, 9 inches.

A. grandiflorum. Similar to the above, but generally longer lived and will reach 18 inches high when well established.

A. iberideum. Prostrate growth. The greyish leaves are nearly circular. Small clusters of white flowers in May, 4 inches.

A. Warley Rose. One of the most popular of rock garden plants. Covered with round heads of deep pink flowers in April and May, 6 inches. Must be increased by cuttings.

A. Warley Ruber. A deeper colour than the above, but not such a good habit.

AGATHEA. A shrubby blue daisy from South Africa. Needs a light sandy soil and a position in full sun. Though not really hardy, it is so easily raised from cuttings that it is well worth growing. Produces a good show of flowers throughout the summer and on into the autumn months. A few cuttings put into a pot of very sandy soil and kept in a frame during the winter will provide replacements after a hard winter.

A. coelestis. Clear true blue with golden centre. One year old plants are about 9 inches high, but those that have managed to survive several winters will attain 18 inches or more.

AJUGA. Bugle. Gout Ivy. With no claim to great beauty they are invaluable carpeters, growing in any soil and even manage to flower in damp, shady sites. Spread very quickly by means of runners and should not be planted too near less vigorous plants or they will choke them.

A. crispa. A dwarf variety with crinkled leaves that have a bluish metallic sheen. Spreads slowly. Spikes of blue flowers in June, 4 inches.

A. reptans purpurea. Leaves of a reddish purple. Spikes of blue flowers in May and June, 6 inches.

A. reptans variegata. Like the above, but the leaves are variegated with pink and cream.

ALYSSUM. Madwort. Gold Dust. A large family of

hardy annuals and perennials, only a few of which are worth a place in the rock garden, but those few include some of our showiest spring flowers. They like a light well drained soil, not too rich and preferably containing lime. The more sun they have the better, and plenty of space is advisable as a well established patch of old plants is a magnificent sight and gives a greater display of bloom than the same area planted up with young plants. Increased by seed, except the double flowered variety.

A. idaeum. Dwarf prostrate silver leaves. Heads of yellow flowers produced in May till July, 2 inches. Not an easy plant, will do best in a well drained position such as provided by a scree.

A. montanum. Semi-prostrate species with green leaves and mustard yellow flowers in summer, 6 inches. Rather too rampant for the amount of flower, but useful in a rock wall.

A. saxatile. Strong yellow flowers in April to May, 9 inches. The well known Gold Dust used for bedding.

A. s. compactum. A neater growing form of the above and more suitable for rock gardens.

A. s. citrinum. A lemon yellow form. When raising from seed, it is advisable to flower the young plants to make sure they have come true to colour, specially if they are intended for a position where the strong yellow of the ordinary form would not look well.

A. s. Dudley Neville. An apricot flowered hybrid.

A. s. flore pleno. A double flowered form which holds its flowers longer than the singles. Cuttings are best taken with a heel just after the plant has flowered.

A. spinosum roseum. An uncommon little shrublet. The flowers are a washy pink and of no particular value, but after they fall the stems that remain harden into spines which give the plant a silvery white appearance all through the winter, 12 inches.

ANDROSACE. Rock Jasmine. True Alpine plants that need care during the damp weather in winter which makes them rot off at ground level. They must be planted in very well drained soil, and most of them like lime and need a position in full sun. The majority of them have greyish green leaves covered with silver hairs, these hairs are for protection from the dry cold of intense frosts in their native habitat, but are a drawback in our climate as they hold the moisture in winter which is the plant's worst enemy. A sheet of glass arranged over the plants during winter will help them to survive, and a layer of coarse limestone chippings around them assists good drainage. The plants may be divided, but better results are obtained from cuttings. Single rosettes of the current season's growth are put in a sand frame and root very easily; when it is required to get a large patch quickly, the rooted cuttings may be planted out two or three together, and each rosette should give a flower head the following season.

A. arachnoidea. Small rosettes. Heads of white flowers on a short stem in May, 1 inch. Best grown in the scree or alpine house.

A. carnea. An exception to the usual rule for the family in that it does not tolerate lime, and likes protection from full sun. Green leaves. Clear pink flowers in July, 2 inches.

A. Chamaejasme. Leaves rather pointed, but in the usual little rosettes. Flowers white in May and June, 3 inches.

A. lactaea. Stiff shiny leaves. White starry flowers on branching stems in June, 3 inches. Sets seed freely which make nice little plants in a year.

A. lanuginosa. A trailing species with lovely silver leaves, planted above a large rock where it can fall down in a mass, it is at its best. Flower heads of mauvish pink are produced throughout the summer on 6 inch stems, but as these too are prostrate, the whole plant does not reach that height.

A. l. Leitchlinii. As the above, with white flowers that have a distinct red eye.

A. l. Lissadel variety. Like A. lanuginosa, but slightly larger in every way.

A. pyrenaica. Dense little cushions of tiny grey green rosettes that are covered with little white flowers in April. A plant for the alpine house rather than the rock garden. Its tendency to go brown in patches if not treated with great care is a challenge to the ardent gardener, so that a healthy specimen of more than four inches across is a tribute to the grower.

A. sarmentosa. One of the best for the rock garden, being hardier than the usual varieties, spreads quickly and has produced some fine named hybrids. Umbels of pink flowers from May to July, 6 inches.

A. s. var. Chumbyi. As above. Flowers rosy red.

A. s. var. Watkinsii. Deep pink.

A. s. var. Yunnanense. Strong pink, and rather larger than the type.

A. sempervivoides. Rosettes free from hairs, so the plant is better able to resist damp. Flowers bright pink in April, 3 inches.

ANEMONE. Wind Flower. Only a few of this family are suitable for the rock garden, most being woodland plants. They generally look best if planted in combination with a low carpeter such as Thymus serpyllum. Soil should be good and fairly deep, and the position open but not too scorched in summer. Those varieties that are raised from seed, will do best if the seed is sown as soon as it is collected, at which time it will germinate well and very quickly. Keep a regular watch for the ripening seeds as they seem quite firmly fixed one day, and a couple of days later it has all blown away.

A. Pulsatilla. Ferny foliage, the plant forms quite a large clump with age. Rich purple flowers with bright yellow anthers, the outer side of the petals is covered with silvery hairs. April and May, 12 inches. There are some very poor forms with washy coloured flowers, so when collecting seed, only save from plants with the best coloured flowers.

A. P. alba. A white form of the above.

A. P. rubra. Flowers wine red.

A. vernalis. A very beautiful white flower that is covered with silky hairs on the outside. The anthers are really golden. March, 4 inches. Both this and A. Pulsatilla produce fluffy seed heads which add greatly to the attraction of the plants.

ANTENNARIA. Cat's Ear. Close carpeters which are very useful for paving or as ground cover through which taller plants may push their way. Will thrive in ordinary soil, provided it is not too wet. Easily increased by division.

A. dioica rosea. Neat dark green foliage. Flowers small pink in June on 6 inch stems.

A. d. tomentosa. Leaves more attractive being silvery, but the little white flowers are very dull.

ANTHEMIS. Camomile. This herb needs a poor, light soil or it becomes too rank. Given a place in full sun, it makes a good background for spring bulbs planted between the clumps. Increased by division.

A. aizoon. Beautiful mat of silver leaves. Pure white flowers in summer, 4 inches.

ANTHYLLIS. A prostrate little plant, not unlike a clover, to which it is allied. In ordinary light soil in a sunny position it will spread into a large plant. Increased from cuttings of soft side shoots in summer.

A. montana rubra. A mat of grey green leaves. Flowers crimson in June, 3 inches.

ANTIRRHINUM. Snapdragon. The only one that is commonly grown in rock gardens, needs very well drained positions in rock crevices. Is easily raised from seed.

A. Asarina. Prostrate spreading stems with ivy-shaped leaves. The flowers which are like those of the bedding Antirrhinum are borne singly along the stem and are clear citron yellow. Flowers all summer. Not always hardy, but easily raised from seed, self-sown seedlings often appear in the very places they look best, such as a crack in a large rock, where planting is almost impossible.

AQUILEGIA. Columbine. Some of these well known plants are very suitable for the rock garden, specially the lower growing species. The commoner types should be avoided as they seed too freely and tend to become a nuisance. Ordinary soil, and positions in sun or semi-shade. Easily grown from seed, but home-saved seed is often a failure as the different varieties cross very easily, and, of course, it is the commoner types that predominate in the resultant hybrids.

A. alpina. Clear blue flowers. Suitable for naturalizing where there is plenty of space, 18 inches.

A. escalcarata. A dwarf plant with delicate ferny leaves. Small flowers of an unusual shade of brownish purple, 6 inches.

A. glandulosa. Beautiful clear blue flowers with the central petals white, 12 inches.

A. longissima. An attractive species with yellow flowers that have very long spurs in May, 18 inches.

A. pyrenaica. A dwarfer form of A. alpina.

ARABIS. Rock Cress. A large family of which a few are invaluable in the rock garden, while many others are worthless little weeds. Very useful in walls as it thrives in hot, dry situations, and poor soil with plenty of lime suits it best. Increased by division or cuttings, some species are best raised from seed.

A. albida. Low mats of green leaves which spread very quickly. Valuable because of the earliness of its white flowers, 9 inches.

A. a. flore pleno. Like the above in habit, but the double white flowers are a great improvement, and hold longer, though coming into bloom a little later. April to June, 9 inches.

A. a. variegata. Leaves liberally marked with yellow. Flowers single white.

A. blepharophylla. A doubtful perennial easily raised from seed. Flowers a rich purplish pink in May, 8 inches. Collect seed only from the best coloured plants, some are rather washy.

A. rosea. Pale pink flowers. A disappointing plant that can easily be replaced by a pink Aubrietia.

A. Sturri. Rosettes of shiny little leaves. White flowers, 4 inches.

ARENARIA. Sandwort. The members of this family vary in their requirements and are best treated separately.

A. balearica. A close carpet of little green leaves that will clothe the bare rock face, if planted in a moist position in semi-shade. Covered with tiny white flowers in May and June which accounts for its popular name of " Spilt Milk ", 1 inch.

A. montana. Forms a loose mat of wiry stems that scramble over rocks and through small shrubs. Huge white flowers in June and July, 6 inches. Needs light soil and a sunny position. Easily raised from seed.

A. purpurascens. Shiny green leaves, lilac starry flowers in June, 2 inches. Not showy enough to be grown alone, but makes a good carpet for the weaker growing early bulbs.

A. tetraquetra. The leaves are arranged in an unusual manner that are its only claim to fame. Best used as a dwarf carpeter. Tiny white flowers in May.

ARMERIA. Thrift. Form pleasing green cushions that look quite at home between large rocks. They do best in a light sandy soil in full sun. Increased by division early in the year, if attempted in the autumn, many of the pieces will rot off.

A. caespitosa. The aristocrat of the family. Little hummocks of grey green narrow leaves. Large flower heads of silver pink on 1 inch stems in April. Very suitable for scree or alpine house.

A. corsica. The leaves are narrower than those of the ordinary Thrift. Flowers an unusual terra-cotta shade. Produces a succession of flowers from June till August, 6 inches.

A. maritima. The native Sea Pink frequently found on our coast. The white form is also to be found. For garden work it is generally better to obtain one of the named hybrids, as the colours are uniform and stronger. May and June, 6 inches.

A. m. Laucheana. A bright pink, free flowering form.

A. m. Vindictive. Good strong crimson flowers over a long period.

ARTEMISIA. Wormwood aromatic herbs of a shrubby nature which need light sandy soil in full sun. Increased by heel cuttings in late summer.

A. pedemontana. Grown for its lovely silver grey leaves which form a dense mound 3–6 inches deep, and makes a good contrast for deep coloured flowers growing near it. The flowers are not of any value and spoil the carpeting effect.

ASPERULA. Woodruff. Low growing plants with narrow leaves. Most species prefer semi-shade. Increased by division or cuttings early in the year.

A. Gussoni. Makes fat little green cushions covered with pink flowers in May. Does best in sun, but needs the deep root run provided by a scree.

A. hirta. Makes underground shoots that run through stoney soil and covers a large area. The little white flowers fade to pink. July and August, 3 inches.

A. suberosa. One of the favourite rock plants. The grey, woolly leaves need protection from winter damp. The flowers are clusters of delicate pink trumpets in June, 3 inches.

ASTER. The dwarf Michaelmas Daisies can be used to good account in the rock garden as well as many other species of the family. All need a good garden soil to flower well, and the stronger growers benefit from frequent division.

A. alpinus. Mauve daisy flowers in May and June, 6 inches.

A. diplostephioides. Strong basal rosette of dark green leaves. The large purple flowers with distinct yellow eye are borne singly on 9 inch stems in June.

A. pygmaeus. The named hybrids include shades of mauve, pinks and lilac. All flower in autumn.

Diana. Soft pink, 9 inches.

Julia. Lilac, 10 inches.

Margaret Rose. Bright rose pink, 9 inches.

Remembrance. Lilac, 12 inches.

Victor. Pale lavender blue, 6 inches.

AUBRIETIA. Purple Rock Cress. One of the most universally grown of all rock plants. To be seen at its best, a position in full sun is needed, and the soil should be light and well drained, containing lime. To keep the plants looking neat for many years, it is necessary to cut them back, this should be done directly after flowering, do not be afraid to cut them hard—they will look quite bare for a couple of weeks and then make nice green mounds for winter, instead of the straggling patches so often seen. For ordinary purposes, division will give enough plants, but cuttings can also be taken. Named varieties are many, and a good strain of seed will provide many worth while colours, from which the best should be selected. Never waste good space on bad plants when there are so many beautiful ones from which to choose.

Carnival. Very large, deep violet purple.

Church Knowle. Pale blue with white eye.

Crimson King. Large, red purple.

Dr. Mules. Dark blue purple.

A. gloriosa. Very large, rose pink.

Gurgedyke. Strong red purple.

J. S. Baker. Blue with distinctive white eye.

Lavender Beauty. Pale lavender.

Lloyd Edwards. Deep violet.

Red Carnival. Good strong red.

A. rosea splendens. Low growing, lilac pink.

A. variegata aurea. Leaves edged with golden yellow. Flowers pale mauve.

A. variegata argentea. Leaves beautifully marked with white, very neat growth. Flowers pale mauve.

Vindictive. Good strong crimson. Very vigorous grower.

AUBRIETIA
Cut back hard after flowering.
JULY

seeding

CUT BACK HARD

End of August ....   *green again.*

BELLIS. Daisy. Though not the correct type of plant for the rock garden, few people can resist putting in a patch here and there to give a little extra colour. They are greedy plants and need a good rich soil to look well. Easily increased by division and some come true from seed.

B. perennis. Named hybrids from seed.

Dresden China. Miniature pale pink buttons.

Rob Roy. Deep red, double flowers.

BELLIUM. Suitable as a little carpeter that will not swamp small plants. Will grow in ordinary light soil and is increased by division.

B. minutum. White daisy flowers which fade through pink to red are produced all summer, 1 inch.

CALAMINTHA. A charming little plant of shrubby growth with aromatic leaves, rather like the Thymes, but with much larger flowers. Light sandy soil and full sun are needed. Cuttings in pure sand in spring root quite easily, but plants from seed are a better shape.

C. alpina. Purple flowers in June. A neat growing little bush, 6 inches.

C. grandiflora. Coarser growing than the above, and erect habit. Pink flowers in June and July, 12 inches.

CALANDRINIA. Is a perennial that often dies off in a cold, wet winter, and, as it is so quickly and easily raised from seed, it is best to sow a few seeds each spring for flowering the same year. It needs very well drained soil, and is suitable for the scree, as it does not get too rampant.

C. umbellata. The large magenta flowers make a great show at a time when colour is scarce in the rock garden. July to September, 6 inches.

CALCEOLARIA. Need a soil that does not dry out during the summer, yet must not be waterlogged in winter. Partial shade, but of course away from the drip from trees or shrubs.

C. Darwini. Not easy to grow, but must be mentioned because of the striking flowers, these are yellow and the bag has a deep maroon mark on it and the lip is pure white, like a bar of wax.

C. polyrrhiza. Spreads by creeping underground roots. Flowers deep yellow on 6 inch stems that rise from the mat of leaves. July.

C. tenella. Bright green carpet in semi-shade. If planted beside a large rock, it will quickly spread to cover the whole area, and the part that is on bare rock will survive a hard winter better than that in soil. Yellow flowers lightly speckled with crimson, 2 inches.

CAMPANULA. Bell Flower. Invaluable plants for many purposes, they do best in a good well drained soil, with a little leaf mould added. They prefer a sunny position, but some will make a good show in the semi-shade also. Most of them spread by underground shoots and the clumps can be divided in spring when growth has started, some are best raised from seed, but named varieties will not breed true. Only a selection of the very many species grown will be given here.

C. Allionii. Prostrate plant best suited for the scree. Large, deep blue purple bells. June to August, 3 inches.

C. arvatica. A really dwarf species, best for scree or alpine house, as it gets lost among rampant plants. Upstanding, starry flowers of deep violet, 2 inches.

C. Bellardi (*pusilla, cochlearifolia*. All these names are found in trade catalogues for the dwarf Harebell). Quite hardy, and able to stand the wear and tear of life in a paved walk. Small, lavender blue bells, 4 inches.

C. B. alba. White flowered form of the above.

C. B. Miranda. Flowers much larger of pale silvery blue.

C. carpatica. Very easy to grow, rather too large for the small rock garden, but excellent in a mixed flower border. Blue, 12 inches.

C. c. alba. White form of the above.

C. c. Isobel. Large, flat saucers of dark, shiny purple. June and July, 9 inches.

C. c. Riverslea. Deep blue, erect cups.

C. c. White Star. Pure white cups, a better variety than C. carpatica alba.

C. garganica. Grows as a flat rosette which sends out prostrate stems covered with starry flowers over a long season, starting in June, 3 inches.

C. g. hirsuta. With greyish, woolly leaves.

C. g. W. H. Paine. A beautiful distinct variety. The bright violet blue flowers have clearly marked white centres.

C. Kewensis. A beautiful miniature hybrid which is best grown in a pan in the alpine house. Dark blue, starry flowers, 3 inches.

C. nitida alba. Dark, shiny leaves. Stiff, erect stems 9 inches high with pure white flowers in July. Must be lifted and replanted frequently, as they tend to wear themselves out with much flowering. Increase by planting out young side shoots singly into good soil.

C. Portenschlagiana (*muralis*). The most useful of all the campanulas. Will flower in sun or semi-shade in almost any soil. The trailing spikes of violet blue bells are produced all through the summer and far into the autumn, 6 inches.

C. Poscharskyana. Makes strong clumps of green leaves. The flowers are lavender blue stars borne on long trailing red stems. Excellent on a wall where the flower stems press against the stone and radiate in all directions covering a large area. Summer into autumn, 8 inches.

C. pulla. A beautiful little plant with pendulous blooms of metallic purple, that are very large for the size of the plant. Good for the scree or alpine house. June and July, 3 inches.

C. pulloides. A hybrid of the above, and much larger and easier to grow. Flowers deep violet blue, 4 inches.

C. Raineri. Large, blue cups on very short stems, leaves grey green. June and July.

C. rotundifolia. The native Harebell, a good form with deep blue flowers is well worth a place in the garden.

C. Stansfieldii. A hybrid with pale green leaves that form a loose mat. The flowers are clear lavender and have very pointed teeth edging the narrow bell, 4 inches.

C. turbinata. Hairy, greyish leaves. Large, blue flowers. Summer, 9 inches. Like a dwarfer, C. carpatica.

C. t. albescens. A silvery blue counterpart of the above. The two are very effective when planted together.

C. Warleyensis. Double flowers of china blue. July and August, 6 inches. The stems are not strong enough to hold the flowers erect when they are heavy after rain, so a good layer of lime stone chippings or gravel will help to keep the flowers from getting muddied.

CARLINA. A dwarf Thistle that should be planted in very poor soil or it will become too rampant. Interesting because it figures in very many of the designs for carving and embroidery found in alpine districts.

C. acaulis. A flat rosette of prickly leaves with a large, stemless flower in the centre. June.

CERASTIUM. Snow in Summer. A very rampant grower that must be cut back drastically after flowering to keep it within bounds. Any light soil will do for it, and in full sun it gets covered with flower. Divide the plants when they get too straggly.

C. Biebersteinii. Greyish leaves. White flowers in May, 6 inches.

C. tomentosum. Leaves very woolly and neater than the former.

CHEIRANTHUS. Wallflower. The ones suited for the rock garden are neater growing than the well known bedding wallflower. They need well drained soil that contains lime, and a sunny position. Though really perennials, it is best to keep a succession of young plants coming on, as they are very liable to get eelworm, and when this appears the infected plants must be pulled up at once and burned.

C. Harpur Crewe. Double golden yellow flowers in spring, 15 inches. If cut back after flowering, will give a second crop of bloom.

C. Moonlight. Clear lemon yellow, 9 inches.

C. mutabilis. Flowers mixed bronze and purple, 9 inches.

C. Rufus. Beautiful fiery red-orange, 9 inches.

CHRYSANTHEMUM. Most of the family are too closely associated with greenhouses and florists to be " right " in the rock garden, but one in particular deserves a place.

C. Mawii. Silvery grey foliage. Flowers soft pink on wiry stems in summer and autumn, 12–15 inches. Seed will give a variety of shades of pink, mostly with dark eyes; if the best of these are marked when in flower, cuttings can be taken, and also seed saved of the best strain. Light sandy soil in full sun.

CODONOPSIS. Related to the Campanulas, but with a long, fleshy root. Grow it in light soil in full sun. Much beloved by slugs in spring. Easily raised from seed.

C. ovata. Prostrate stems bearing pale blue bells, the inside of which are marked with dark veins.

CONVOLVULUS. Bindweed. Beware of these—any with fat, white roots should be left for the owners of very large gardens. Beautiful no doubt, but they just cannot be kept within bounds. The shrubby ones are safe, but rather delicate.

C. Cneorum. Shrubby with silver leaves. Large, pink flowers, 18 inches.

C. Mauretanicus. Trailing stems of periwinkle blue flowers July to September, 9 inches. In a well drained soil protected from hard winter weather, this will survive many seasons.

CORTUSA. A useful little carpeter that will grow in any

soil or situation and is quickly increased by division. With all that in its favour, it would be unjust to expect beauty of flower.

C. squalida. The flowers it has are inconspicuous, the foliage is a bronzy green, 1 inch.

CORYDALIS. Fumitory. These plants have a deceptively delicate appearance for in reality they are very sturdy. Good ordinary soil, will thrive in sun or half-shade. Increase bulbous species by division, others by seed.

C. lutea. Ferny leaves with spurred flowers of canary yellow all through the summer. Establishes itself very prettily in walls, but is far too prolific in production of seedlings, 9 inches.

C. Solida. The ferny leaves have a grey blue tinge which make a good colour scheme with the mauve pink flowers in April, 6 inches. The whole plant dies down after flowering till the following season.

COTYLEDON. Many of these are also called Echeveria and are not hardy. The one mentioned here is hardy and will grow in sun or semi-shade, and likes good sandy loam, increased by division or seed.

C. simplicifolia. Fleshy leaves. Pendulous racemes of clear yellow flowers. April to June, 6 inches.

CYANANTHUS. Not very easy to grow. They need a lime free soil, and that difficult combination of a plentiful supply of moisture in summer while being well drained in winter. Protect from slugs. Cuttings taken early in the year give the best results.

C. Farreri. Soft green mat of small leaves. Deep blue flowers in July and August, 6 inches.

C. lobatus. Leaves larger and a deeper green. Flowers dark blue.

CYNOGLOSSUM. Hound's Tongue. Best raised from seed every second year, as the plants are not very long lived. Full sun and well drained soil.

C. nervosum. Greyish leaves. Flowers like a large Forget-me-not of the most intense blue. In another more usual colour, the plant would not be worth a place among the alpines, but coming as it does in late summer, it justifies the trouble of raising new plants frequently, 12 inches.

DELPHINIUM. Of the many small growing species listed in catalogues, few are really worth the trouble needed to protect them from the constant attacks of slugs. Good garden loam and a position in the sun. Increased by seed.

> **D. nudicaule.** Orange scarlet. June and July, 12 inches. Has fleshy root stocks. Disappears completely in winter.

> **D. tatsiense.** Delicate branching stems of brilliant blue flowers. Save seed from the best coloured plants —they vary very much. July and August, 18 inches.

DIANTHUS. Pink. Few families provide so many delightful and easy plants for the rock garden as the Dianthus. There is a large range of sizes and colours to be had, and varying types of growth to suit different positions. The soil should be gritty and contain lime, and the habit and flowering of the plants is best when they are in full sun. When a special named variety is wanted, increase by cuttings or division, but seed will give attractive mixtures from which the best can be selected for planting out.

> **D. Allwoodii alpinus Apollo.** Neat little tufted plant. Very free flowering all through the summer. Good pink, 4 inches.

> **D. A. a. Mars.** As the above, but the flowers are a strong crimson.

> **D. alpinus.** Deep rose. June and July, 3 inches. Best in scree or alpine house.

> **D. arvernensis.** Neat, low growing foliage, makes lovely cushions in a paving or on a wall. Small pink flowers in May and June, 3 inches.

> **D. caesius.** The Cheddar Pink. This species and its many hybrids are obliging plants that make good grey green cushions and have flower stems 6 inches high.

A tiny lily pool bordered by moisture-loving
plants, including astilbes, and a maple.

This shows what can be done even in a small
suburban garden.

Flowers can be double or single, and the colour ranges from white through pink to deepest red.

D. callizonus. A dwarf with very large pink flowers in June. Best in the scree or alpine house.

D. deltoides. Comes true from seed and is best raised that way. The leaves are small and either green or reddish brown. Flowers strong pink with tiny flecks of crimson. Summer, 6 inches. Named hybrids in white and red can also be grown.

D. graniticus. Trailing habit. Pink flowers in summer.

D. microlepis. The narrow leaves form little " hedge-hogs " which are studded with little pink flowers in May. Looks most attractive in pans for the alpine house, though well able to survive in the open. Its chief enemy is moss, which grows up through the clumps and chokes them. Good drainage and a loose layer of stone chippings help to stop this trouble.

D. neglectus. Narrow green leaves. Flowers carmine with the reverse of the petals buff. June and July, 4 inches. Best in the scree.

D. superbus. Ragged little flowers with a very strong scent, for which the plant is well worth growing.

D. sylvestris. Grassy tufts. Pink flowers on branching stems 12 inches high. One of the few with no scent.

Some of the garden hybrids usually grown in the flower border can be included, but avoid any that have heavy formal growth.

DOUGLASIA. Makes cushions of grey green shoots like miniature fir trees. Well drained deep sandy soil in full sun. Increase by cuttings or seed.

D. Vitaliana. Heads of golden flowers in spring, 3 inches. Suitable for the scree.

DRABA. Whitlow Grass. A race of rather dull little plants which look too near the border-line of being weak-growing weeds to be popular. Sandy soil in full sun. Seed or division.

D

D. aizoides. Green, thorny looking rosettes. Golden yellow flowers in spring, 3 inches.

D. pyrenaica (synonym : *Petrocallis pyrenaica*). Spreading tufts of small leaves, covered with pale lilac, scented flowers in spring, 1 inch.

DRYAS. Mountain Avens. Useful for the good carpet of strong green leaves as well as the flowers and attractive seed heads. Sandy soil in sun or semi-shade. Increase by cuttings or division.

D. octopetala. White flowers with golden anthers from June to August, followed by fluffy seed heads, 6 inches.

D. o. grandiflora. A freer flowering form. Which also roots more readily from cuttings.

EDRAIANTHUS. Wahlenbergia. Closely allied to the Campanulas. They need a well drained, stony soil and a sunny position. Increased by seed and cuttings. Keep a watch out for slugs, specially if seed is to be saved—the slugs seem to like to eat the whole of the seed case before it ripens.

E. serpyllifolia. Slender prostrate stems, ending in large, satiny, purple bells. May. Lovely in the scree or in pans.

E. tenuifolia. Narrow grey leaves. Pale lavender bells on slender stems. June.

EPILOBIUM. Willow Herb. There is one member of this family of strong growing herbs, of which the Rose Bay is the best known, that is suitable for the rock garden. Stony soil, rich in humus, and an ample supply of moisture is needed for the plant to spread happily. Sun or semi-shade. Can be increased by division in spring, cuttings or seed.

E. Fleischeri. Useful because it flowers in August, when most of the colour has gone from the rock garden. Soft pink and rosy claret, 9 inches.

ERIGERON. Fleabane. Aster-like plants, the low growing ones being suitable for the rock garden, and even those generally planted in the flower borders can be used where space allows. Ordinary garden soil in sun. Division or seed.

E. leiomerus. A dwarf little daisy. Pale violet flowers. June, 3 inches.

E. mucronatus. A wiry little plant, covered all summer with pink and white daisies. Excellent for seeding itself into the cracks of rocks, walls or paving, yet easily removed if not required, 6 inches.

ERINUS. The perfect little plant for the rock garden or seeding itself on old walls. Light, poor soil and full sun are needed to get the best results. If grown in rich soil, many of the plants will die in the winter through bad drainage. Seed; named varieties will not come true when planted near other forms, with which they cross freely.

E. alpinus. Neat little rosette of leaves and spikes of flowers growing from 3–6 inches high, according to the situation. Mauvish pink.

E. a. albus. A white form of the above.

E. a. Abbottswood Pink. A pretty clear pink.

E. a. Dr. Haneele. Rich ruby red.

ERITRICHIUM. Rare and beautiful, gives the best results in scree or alpine house. Lime free, well drained soil, in a sunny position. Seed gives the best results, though plants can also be carefully divided.

E. nanum. Too difficult except for the specialist.

E. strictum. More vigorous. Grey leaves. China blue flowers on short stems in summer, 3 inches.

ERODIUM. Heron's Bill. While never making a blaze of colour, these plants give a steady succession of bloom over a long period. The whole plant is generally attractive in its type of growth, and the foliage is aromatic. They thrive in light, sandy soil and do best in full sun. Increased by seeds or cuttings.

E. chamaedryoides roseum. Flat rosettes of small, green leaves. Covered all summer with pink, starry flowers, 2 inches.

E. chrysanthum. Ferny, grey green leaves. Pale yellow flowers. June–September, 6 inches.

E. corsicum. Round leaves with scalloped edges. Pale pink flowers in summer, 4 inches.

E. macradenum. Ferny foliage. Pink flowers with dark blotches on the lower petals, 6 inches.

ERYSIMUM. Much confusion exists in the naming of these plants, the simplest method is to realize that they are often classed with the Cheiranthus, and leave the Botanists to worry about the slight differences that divide them. Light soil containing lime and a sunny position are all they need. Raise new plants by seed or cuttings to replace those that have become too woody or straggling with age.

E. linifolium. Wiry plant with narrow leaves, and covered with lilac flowers in summer, 9 inches.

E. pulchellum. Tufted growth with yellow flowers, 4 inches.

E. rupestre. Spreading mats of dark green leaves. Yellow flowers, 4 inches.

ERYTHRAEA. Centaury. A lime-hating plant that does well planted among Gentians. Well drained peat soil. Increased by division or seed.

E. diffusa. Leaves are a yellowish green. Flowers a clear clean pink in June, 3 inches.

FRANKENIA. Sea Heath. Used for paving and the sides of paths. The foliage is small and heath-like. Easily increased by planting out the rooted shoots which spread all round the plant.

F. laevis. Little, stemless, pink flowers, all over the young shoots in summer, 3 inches.

GAZANIA. Not alpines and not quite hardy, yet these brilliant plants seem to be claiming a place in rock gardens of the present day. They are natives of South Africa, and combine long flowering with a full range of fiery colours. Very sunny positions in light, sandy soil give them the best chance of coming through the winter. Cuttings root very easily in sand, and many interesting hybrids can be raised from seed.

G. Fletcherii. Lemon yellow.

G. montana. White with black markings.

G. splendens. Trailing habit. Brilliant orange, the centre is marked with black and white arranged in a regular pattern.

Many named hybrids in shades of red, yellow, orange and deep bronze. Nearly all have the centre of the large daisy flowers marked with darker colours often in combination with pure white.

GENTIANA. Of the very many Gentians that have been introduced into this country, only a specialist would want to grow more than a selection of species. Most of them thrive in a lime free soil, and in most gardens it is necessary to make up a special bed to suit their requirements. For this, a compost of loam, peat and coarse sand will be needed, into which the trailing species can send down their long, fleshy roots. Summer drought is their enemy, though they like to get plenty of sun. Increased by seed and careful division.

G. acaulis. One of the best known, forming close hummocks that grow in most garden soils. The huge trumpets of Prussian blue have very short stems. The main flowering season is April and May, though occasional flowers will appear during the winter, 4 inches.

G. Farreri. Mats of grass-like leaves. Large trumpet flowers with stripes on the outside of shades of blue, inside is shaded to white. September and October.

G. lagodechiana. Very like G. Hascombensis and G. septemfida, in most gardens it is enough to grow any one of these. From a central root stock, long trailing stems radiate, these produce many blue flowers in late summer. Grow well in any good soil that does not get too dry in summer. Keep the plants protected from slugs, and resist the temptation of dividing them as soon as they get established—large plants give by far the best results. The seedlings are very small and hard to handle at the first pricking out, the best ones will give an occasional bloom in the second year.

G. sino-ornata. Type of growth like G. Farreri, but more rampant. When growing well, it makes a thick mat of trailing stems that in September throw up a mass of huge, blue trumpets, that continue until winter sets in.

G. verna. The beautiful little flower that figures in Swiss post cards. Most easily established if young seedling plants are used, as so many divided plants have had many of the very long roots damaged. Brilliant blue upstanding flowers in April and May, 2 inches.

GERANIUM. Crane's Bill. The smaller growing species are a great addition to the rock garden, having pretty foliage as well as flowers that bloom over a long period. Grown in rather poor, sandy soil in a sunny position they are seen at their best ; when treated too well, they get soft and leafy and the flowers are often hidden by a mass of lush leaves. Most can be raised from seed, named varieties are increased by putting in cuttings of side shoots into a sand frame in early summer.

G. argenteum. Beautiful silver leaves. Large, rose pink flowers in June, 6 inches.

G. cinereum. Rather like the above. The pink flowers have dark veining and there is a white form.

G. napuligerum (*Farreri*). Pale pink flowers with large, black anthers. June and July, 4 inches.

G. sanguineum. Long, branching stems with large, magenta flowers in May and continuing till September, 9 inches.

G. s. lancastriense. As the above, but with clear pink flowers.

G. Traversi. Lovely grey green leaves and pale pink flowers. Keep it in poor soil, if growing rampantly it loses all its charm.

GEUM. Avens. Most of these are best for the flower border, but where space is available, a few may be planted because of their long flowering season, and sturdy, green leaves in winter.   Any good garden soil, and they will flower in sun or semi-shade.   Increase by division or seed.

G. Borisii.   Brilliant orange flowers, 9 inches.

G. montanum.   Large, golden flowers, 6 inches.

G. rivale.   Tall stems carrying many hanging heads of old rose flowers, does well in the semi-shade, 12 inches.

GLOBULARIA.   Very useful low growing carpeters. Well drained loam in sunny positions.   Division of the runners, or cuttings from the more compact growing species.

G. bellidifolia.   Neat little dark green, shiny leaves. Round heads of powder blue flowers in June, 3 inches. An excellent carpeter for small bulbs.

G. incanescens.   Leaves roundish and grey green. Tufted growth which sends out short runners.   Fluffy heads of blue flowers, 2 inches.

G. tricosantha.   Spreads quickly, covering the ground with a close carpet of shiny leaves, even in a shady position.   The blue flowers are on 6 inch stems.

GYPSOPHILA.   Low growing forms of the garden Gypsophila.   Light, sandy soil and full sun.   Comes easily from cuttings taken in early summer.

G. Fratensis.   Makes large hummocks of pale green leaves.   Clear pink flowers in June and July, 3 inches.

G. repens.   So like the above that many nurserymen list them as the same plant.

G. Sundermanni.   White flowers on branching stems, 12 inches.

HABERLEA.   Plants for the cool side of a rock, needing lime free soil and protection from winter damp.   Side shoots pulled from the old plant will root quickly, or leaf cuttings can be taken.

H. rhodopensis.   Rosettes of thick, green leaves.   Sprays of mottled, lilac flowers in May, 6 inches.

H. virginalis.   White flowers.

HELIANTHEMUM.   Rock Rose, Sun Rose.   An invaluable dwarf shrub with large flowers of many shades.   Light soil and full sun suit it best.   Cut the plants back hard each year, directly after flowering and they will not get straggly. Increase by cuttings, seed also grows, but generally gives rather a large number of poor forms.

H. alpestre. A neat growing species with prostrate shoots of small, shiny leaves. Bright yellow flowers. June, 2 inches.

H. lunulatum. Grey green leaves on stiff, woody little stems that make an erect little shrub about 4 inches high, excellent for planting in a trough garden, or to give height in a bowl planted up as a miniature rock garden. Yellow flowers in great profusion in July.

Hybrids. These are many, the double flowered ones hold longer, but do not give nearly such a blaze of colour, though the old Double Red seems to manage to grow in partial shade and even produce flowers in positions where its more glamorous cousin would fade and die.

Ben Alder. Terra Cotta.

Ben Dearg. Rich Flame.

Ben Lawers. Pale Orange.

Ben Lomond. Rose Madder.

Ben Nevis. Yellow with orange eye.

Ben Venue. Huntsman Pink.

HELICHRYSUM. Everlasting Flower. Well drained soil in sun, though some will do in semi-shade. Spreads quickly, carpeting the ground with small leaves, divide the plants in early spring.

H. bellidioides. Rampant carpeter. White flowers, 6 inches.

H. bracteatum. Golden yellow flowers, 12 inches.

H. frigidum. Miniature leaves. White flowers, 2 inches. Looks well filling a pan in the alpine house.

H. trinerve. Another good carpeter with white flowers in spring, 6 inches.

HEUCHERA. Really best in the flower garden, but where space can be found for a few of the red ones, they are a great help in providing colour in the later part of the summer, when things look rather drab. Rich garden soil. Side shoots pulled off and rooted in sand, make better shaped plants than ordinary division of roots.

H. Pluie de Feu.

H. sanguinea.

H. splendens. All good red varieties.

HIERACEUM. Hawk Weed. Watch out that they don't spread too far. Any ordinary soil.

>   **H. aurantiacum.** Heads of deep orange red Dandelion flowers. Spreads very rapidly by runners, but looks well on stone steps in an informal part of the garden. 12 inches.

>   **H. villosum.** Leaves covered with long, white hairs which make the whole plant pale grey. Flowers like large Dandelions of lemon yellow. A striking plant, but too free in setting seed.

HIPPOCREPIS. Horseshoe Vetch. Trailing evergreen, useful on a sunny bank where it can spread over rocks. Ordinary soil, increase by seed.

>   **H. comosa.** Flowers yellow, starting in May and continuing all summer, 3 inches.

HOUSTONIA. Bluets. A tiny plant with low green foliage that makes a " lawn ", if planted in leafy soil that does not dry up during the summer. Needs to be replanted most years.

>   **H. coerulea.** Little blue flowers on 2 inch stems in May and at intervals during the season.

HUTCHINSIA. A bright green carpeter that stays an inch high. Cool soil in partial shade.

>   **H. alpina.** Finely cut leaves, like cress. Heads of tiny white flowers in May.

HYPERICUM. St. John's Wort. A really useful genus, even the dullest have some claim to beauty, and most are neat growing. Light soil in a sunny position. Most of them come true from seed and are most easily raised that way.

>   **H. Coris.** A fine-leaved little bushlet, bearing golden flowers all summer, 6 inches.

>   **H. empetrifolium.** Prostrate, woody stems, covered

D*

with bright yellow flowers in summer, 2 inches. **Lovely** in the scree or alpine house.

H. fragile. Cut back each year after flowering, this bushlet remains neat for many years. Large, golden yellow flowers June till September, 9 inches. Older plants up to 15 inches.

H. olympicum. Flowers like the above, but type of growth less dense.

H. o. citrinum. A lemon yellow form of the above.

H. reptans. Trailing. Best in semi-shade where it keeps moist. Large, yellow flowers, 3 inches.

HYPSELLA. A low growing plant which spreads rapidly by underground stems, provided the slugs don't find it first, and is useful as a carpeter in sun or semi-shade. Good soil with plenty of humus. Increase by division of roots in spring.

H. longifolia. Shiny, green leaves. Striped purplish pink and white. All summer, 1 inch.

IBERIS. Candytuft. Very useful plant, forming evergreen mounds that look well all the year round. Any ordinary garden soil suits them. Will thrive equally well on walls, in paving or in the border. Increase by cuttings or seed.

I. Gibraltarica. Rather disappointing, as it gets very leggy. Flowers in varying shades of purple and mauve. Select only the best colours from a batch of seedlings, 6 inches.

I. sempervirens. Little Gem. Makes a neat little bush. Heads of white flowers in May and June, 6 inches.

I. s. Snowflake. Larger than the above in every way, needs to be cut back every year to keep it compact. Large white flowers in April and May that completely conceal the leaves, and transforms the plant into a sheet of the purest white, 12 inches.

INULA. Another herbaceous plant that is small enough to find a home in the rock garden. Good garden soil, sunny position. Divide when the plants get overcrowded.

I. ensifolia. Narrow, pointed leaves. Large, yellow daisy flowers. July to September, 9 inches.

IRIS. As well as the dwarf bulbous Irises, there are a few that are a great asset in the rock garden. Well drained soil in full sun is needed for the species mentioned here.

I. cristata. A dwarf, much beloved by slugs. Blue flowers marked with gold. April and May, 3 inches. Best for the scree or alpine house.

I. pumila. Like the large Germanica Iris, except for its size. There are many named varieties all excellent for the rock garden, in shades of blue, yellow, purple and white. Heights vary from 3–12 inches. April.

JASIONE. Sheep's-bit Scabious. Grown in poor, light soil where it keeps dwarf, the flowers make a blue haze which is attractive between patches of Rock roses. Seeds itself freely, but does not become a nuisance.

J. perennis. Powder blue flower heads in June. Height varies with the position, 4–12 inches.

LEONTOPODIUM. Edelweiss. A plant from the high Alps, but contrary to popular opinion, it is quite easy to grow. Well drained soil in a sunny position is all it requires. Once established, leave it alone to grow into a large plant.

L. alpinum. Produces the well known Flannel Flowers from June till August, 6 inches.

LEWISIA. These plants come from America, where they grow in the hot, dry districts of California. To succeed here they must have a light, sandy soil, plenty of water in the growing season, all the sun available and dry conditions during the dormant season. All this is naturally most easily provided in the alpine house, where they are seen at their best. Very favoured gardens will be able to give the right conditions, but on the whole, the results are disappointing. Freshly saved seed germinates very well, and the strongest plants will flower in their second season, though the size of bloom will improve in subsequent years.

L. columbiana. Narrow leaves. Umbels of small, pink flowers. May, 6 inches.

L. Heckneri. Flat rosettes of fleshy leaves. Large

flowers with the petals striped white and pink in loose
umbels on stems 9 inches high.

L. Howelli. Like the above in growth. Flowers striped
pink and apricot. May and June.

L. rediviva. Upright, narrow leaves which die down
after flowering season. Flowers are large and cup-
shaped on 2 inch stems, they vary in colour from white
to medium pink.

LINARIA. Toadflax. Beware of these—they look so
small and delicate, but the ones that spread by underground
stems are as vigorous and determined invaders as the worst
weeds. Light, sandy soil, and a position where they may seed
at will is best for the following species, all of which can be
kept under control.

L. alpina. Trailing stems with narrow, grey green
leaves. Little snapdragon flowers of violet and orange.
May to July, 3 inches.

L. a. rosea. Flowers pink and orange.

L. origanifolia. Leaves hairy. Upright growth. Flowers
are large for the size of the stems. Purple and mauve.
Summer, 6 inches.

LINUM. Flax. This family provides some beautiful clean
colours that are very welcome when planning a colour scheme.
Well drained loam and a sunny position. Seed where possible,
but cuttings of L. arboreum.

L. alpinum. Prostrate little blue flax. May and June,
2 inches.

L. arboreum. Neat little bush, covered with large,
clear yellow flowers in May till July, 12 inches. Will
also grow in semi-shade.

L. flavum. Flowers like the above. The stems should
be cut down each year. June, 15 inches. Really more
suitable for the herbaceous border.

L. narbonense. Tall, waving stems bearing huge
flowers of deep blue all summer, 15 inches. Be sure to
get a good coloured strain, the Six Hills variety is
excellent.

L. perenne. Like the above, but with smaller and paler flowers.

LITHOSPERMUM. Gromwell. Small, woody plants that dislike lime. Cuttings put in early in the year give the best results.

> **L. graminifolium.** Long, narrow, dark green leaves. Flower heads are clusters of drooping bells of clear blue. May, 6 inches.
>
> **L. intermedium.** Type of growth like the above, but the full-grown bush is taller.
>
> **L. prostratum.** Heavenly Blue. Continuous succession of brilliant blue flowers along the trailing stems. Will thrive in peat or in a heavy loam, provided it is free of lime.
>
> **L. p. Grace Ward.** A slightly larger form of the above.

LYCHNIS. Catchfly. Obliging little plants that will grow in almost any soil. Come freely from seed, except the double flowered forms, which must be propagated by cuttings.

> **L. alpina.** Rather a dull little plant if seen singly, looks best in large groups. Heads of puce pink in spring, 4 inches.
>
> **L. Lagascae rosea.** Delicate growth and flowers of a good strong pink. May to August, 4 inches.
>
> **L. viscaria flore pleno.** Free flowering, strong pink. May and June, 12 inches. The single form is a poor thing and not worth growing, though the variety *splendens* is a good colour.

LYSIMACHIA. Creeping Jenny. This little creeper will really grow anywhere, even in city gardens. Used in the ordinary rock garden, care must be taken that it does not over-run nearby plants, it grows very quickly.

> **L. nummularia.** Carpet of green leaves studded with bright yellow flowers from June till September, 1 inch.
>
> **L. n. aurea.** A golden-leaved form that is not quite so vigorous.

MAZUS. Low growing carpeter, useful for paving in a

cool, moist situation. Increases quickly and can be divided in spring.

M. reptans. Flowers large for the size of the plant. Pale violet with large golden spot on the petals. May until autumn, 1 inch.

MENTHA. Mint. Only one species will be included here, the majority being unsuitable for rock gardens.

M. Requienii. A close little carpeter that smells strongly of Peppermint when touched. It spreads quickly over the soil in a cool, moist place. Sometimes looks rather sad after a hard winter, but soon greens up again. The flowers are like mauve pin-heads scattered all over the plant.

MORISIA. Needs a gritty soil of considerable depth, where its long tap root can penetrate in search of moisture. The leaves lie flat on the ground, and the whole plant looks just like a green star fish. Propagation is done by putting root cuttings into pure sand.

M. hypogæa. Yellow flowers in spring, 1 inch. Useful in the scree.

MYOSOTIS. Forget-me-not. The ordinary Forget-me-not should be kept out of the rock garden, it is not a rock plant and cannot look like one. The three mentioned here are true perennials, and by their habit of growth can be used. Well drained soil and hard treatment is needed, in rich soil they grow too soft. Propagate by seed.

M. alpestris. Clear blue flowers, dwarf habit, 3 inches.

M. rupicola. Flowers azure blue. Spring, 2 inches.

M. spathulata. Unusual trailing stems. The flowers are pure white, 1 inch.

NEPETA. Catmint. Too large for the small rock garden, but very useful in rock walls or bordering a paved path. Ordinary garden soil, the leaves are a better colour in a dry, sunny position. Cuttings of short basal shoots root quickly.

N. Mussini. Grey green leaves and long spikes of lavender flowers. Keep cut back every year.

There are named varieties with leaves or flowers of different size or colour, but they are seldom an improvement on N. Mussini in length of flower or habit of growth.

ŒNOTHERA. Evening Primrose. These are numerous, but only a few are suitable for the rock garden. Light soil is best, and increase is by seed or cuttings, according to the species.

    Œ. missouriensis. Rather coarse growing. The huge, pale yellow flowers are stemless and produced in succession along the prostrate shoots, which look beautiful trailing over a sunny bank.

    Œ. riparia. A beautiful plant. From a small rosette of basal leaves, long wiry stems grow to about a foot high. These produce many large, yellow flowers all through the summer and early autumn. In windy places, it is advisable to put a few short, twiggy sticks around the plants, to prevent the brittle stems from being broken.

OMPHALODES. The species mentioned need different treatment and are better described separately.

    O. cappadocica. A sturdy plant that thrives in sun or shade, is not fussy about soil, though prefers it cool and leafy, and as well as having a main flowering season in spring, will give occasional blossoms in autumn. Brilliant blue flowers, like large Forget-me-nots, 9 inches.

    O. Luciliæ. Grey, smooth leaves. Flowers pale blue with a faint tinge of pink, the whole very like the flowers in a Dresden china Shepherdess' basket, 4 inches. Keep in well drained, gritty soil, or the leaves get too large and partially hide the flowers. Does very well in the scree or alpine house. To propagate, take off small side shoots in spring and root them in sand.

ONOSMA. Plants with leaves covered with stiff hairs, and clusters of tubular flowers on stems of varied heights. Sandy, well drained soil in sunny positions. Seed gives sturdier plants, the seedlings should be put in their permanent quarters as young as possible, or potted and transferred from them, as they dislike root disturbance.

O. albo-roseum. The flowers are white with a pink mouth that turns deep red with age, 9 inches.

O. stellulatum. Flowers soft primrose yellow, 9 inches.

O. tauricum. Flowers strong yellow, 9 inches.

ORIGANUM. Dittany. Dainty plants with hop-like flowers that need light soil in a sunny position. Increase by careful division in spring.

O. Dictamnus. Woolly, aromatic leaves. Drooping heads of rosy purple flowers in summer, and remaining till autumn, 6 inches. Best grown in the scree.

O. hybridum. Like the above, but larger and sturdier. Flowers purple, 9 inches.

OROBUS. Early flowering plant like a small vetch. Light soil in the sun, though it will flower in semi-shade. Grows freely from seed.

O. vernus (synonym : *Lathyrus vernus*). Flowers are shaded blue and purple. April and May, 9 inches.

OXALIS. Wood Sorrel. Most of the members of this family that are grown in the rock garden form fleshy bulbs, but as they are treated more like herbaceous subjects, they are included here. Many of the innocent carpeters must be looked upon with suspicion, for they multiply as rapidly as the worst weed, and are more difficult to eradicate, but a few are an addition to the beauty of paved walk or rock crevice, so discrimination must be used.

O. adenophylla. Pretty grey green leaves followed by large, delicate pink flowers in May, 3 inches.

O. corniculata. Low growing little plant that seeds itself all over the place and becomes a nuisance if not kept within bounds.

O. enneaphylla. Grows best in rich soil in semi-shade. Large, pearly white flowers in May and June, 3 inches.

O. e. rosea. Like the above. Flowers rose pink.

O. lobata. Rich golden yellow flowers in summer, 2 inches. Dies down in winter.

O. magellanica. A little creeper with white flowers. Does not spread seed, so should be used in preference to O. corniculata.

PAPAVER. Poppy. Only one species is worth growing, and that should be raised frequently from seed, as old plants get ugly and often die off suddenly. Poor, well drained soil is best, and full sun.

P. alpinum. In shades of yellow, apricot, pink, and also white, 3 inches. Lives longer if planted in the scree, and will seed itself about, though never becoming a nuisance.

PAROCHETUS. A carpeter for damp places that spreads quickly, the leaves are like clover. Dig up a lump each winter and put it in a box in a cold greenhouse or frame, the main plant may come through all right, but a supply in reserve is a safeguard.

P. communis. Little Pea flowers of metallic blue all summer, 2 inches.

PENTSTEMON. It is the shrubby species, introduced from America that are most useful for the rock garden. Light loam in a sunny position gives the best results, the presence of peat in the soil is an advantage for some species, but they are not particular. Increased by cuttings which root easily in a sand frame.

P. Roezlii. Dwarf shrublet. Clear ruby red flowers in May and June, 6 inches. Does well in the scree. Commercial stocks are very mixed, and many different plants are sent out under this name.

P. Scouleri. Upright bush covered with spikes of clear lilac in May and June, 12 inches.

P. S. alba. White flowers. Not such a robust grower as the above.

P. Six Hills Hybrid. Shrubby growth of a spreading habit. Rosy purple flowers, 6 inches.

PHLOX. Among the most useful plants for the rock garden. Most of them need a light, well drained soil in full sun, a few prefer semi-shade and a peat soil. The plants send out shoots that root naturally, thus propagation consists of selecting rooted pieces; when large numbers are required, unrooted slips are put in a sand frame.

P. adsurgens. Round, shiny leaves. Shell pink flowers in May, 3 inches. Needs a gritty, peat soil, and protection from slugs in spring.

P. amoena. Low growing, neat plant. Covered with heads of rose pink flowers in April and May, 4 inches. Protect from slugs.

P. Douglasii. Neat cushions of spiny leaves, covered with stemless lilac stars in May, 2 inches.

P. stolonifera. Round leaves. Spreads by long runners. Rose pink flowers in April, 6 inches. Leafy soil in semi-shade.

P. subulata. The best known of the family, often called Rock Phlox. There are many named varieties in different colours.

Brightness. Clear pink with crimson centre.

G. F. Wilson. Mauve blue.

Margery. Good pink.

Samson. Rose pink with red eye.

The Bride. White with pink eye.

POLYGALA. Milkwort. The plants grown in the rock garden vary so much that they are best described separately.

P. calcarea. Neat, low growing leaves. Flowers bright blue in May and June. Grow in full sun, in a light limy loam.

P. Chamaebuxus. Little bush with stiff, shiny leaves. Gorse-like flowers of white and yellow in May, 9 inches. Loam soil, and either sun or shade.

P. c. purpurea. Like the above. Flowers pink and yellow.

P. Vayredae. Narrow leaves, flowers smaller, but stronger colour, being wine purple, 6 inches.

POLYGONUM. Knotweed. Useful plants for covering banks or walls in almost any soil or situation. Just watch that they do not over-run their neighbours. Increase by division.

P. affine. From a carpet of rather untidy leaves, spikes of pink flowers appear in June and continue until late autumn, 9 inches.

P. vaccinifolium. A neater growing plant, the flower spikes are 4 inches high. The leaves turn beautiful shades of yellow and red in autumn.

POTENTILLA. The majority of these are too large and straggly for the rock garden, and are best kept in the flower borders. Ordinary garden soil.

P. nitida. Silvery mat of leaves. Large, rose pink flowers on inch-high stems in summer.

P. Tonguei. Flowers an unusual shade of apricot with a red centre, produced over a long season, starting in June. Will flower in sun or semi-shade, 6 inches.

PRIMULA. A huge family, from which it is difficult to select a few of the most suitable. Their requirements vary greatly, but by excluding the " Bog Primulas " it is possible to say that good loam, frequently containing lime, and sunny positions will get good results.

P. auricula. The less formal varieties are lovely for the rock garden, and patches of mixed seedlings make a great show in spring. Avoid the heavy feeding that is given to produce show blooms as the result would look out of place.

P. Juliae. A creeping Primrose that needs good, rich soil. Does well in shade or sun. Many named hybrids can be got, among the best are : Wanda, Juliana Gloria, Pam, Bunty, Kinlough Beauty. All flower in the early spring, 2–4 inches. Increase by division after flowering when leaf growth is at its most vigorous.

P. marginata. A lovely plant with serrated leaves covered with white mealy-looking substance, clear lavender flowers in April. It is the parent of many beautiful hybrids such as Linda Pope and Marven.

P. pubescens. Not unlike an Auricula. The parent of a large race of garden hybrids, many of them good reds and rich purples. Popular examples are : The

General, Mrs. Wilson, Red Star, Faldonside. Seed collected from these give plants of great interest and variety.

PULMONARIA. Lungwort. Useful plants for positions in sun or semi-shade and any ordinary garden soil. Increased by division.

> **P. angustifolia azurea.** The best, with bright blue flowers in March and April, 8 inches.
>
> **P. saccharata.** Leaves have large white spots on them. Flowers shaded pink and blue.

RAMONDIA. Beautiful plants needing a lime free soil, and a position facing north, but away from drips off trees. Increase by seed which is slow, or division of plants.

> **R. Nataliae.** Rosettes of crinkled leaves. Flowers deep lavender with golden eye. May and June, 6 inches.
>
> **R. pyrenaica.** Dark green rosettes. Erect stems bearing open flowers of clear lilac, 6 inches. Does very well in pots in the alpine house.

RANUNCULUS. Buttercup. Only those introduced from alpine habitats will be mentioned.

> **R. alpestris.** Dwarf white Buttercup, 2 inches.
>
> **R. glacialis.** Grows in screes high up in the Alps. White flowers, 6 inches.
>
> **R. pyrenæus.** Cool, rich soil. White flowers with golden stamens in early summer, 6 inches.

RAOULIA. Dwarf carpeters of exceptionally neat growth. Well drained, sandy soil in full sun is needed for them to be seen at their best. Increased by division.

> **R. australis.** Foliage quite silver. Flowers inconspicuous. Cannot tolerate winter damp.
>
> **R. a. minima.** A minute form of the above.
>
> **R. glabra.** Same type of growth as the above, but with green leaves.

ROSA. The miniature roses look attractive in the rock garden. For soil they need good rich loam, as they are as greedy as their full-sized brothers. Cuttings taken with a heel will root in late summer.

R. Oakington Ruby. Ruby red double flowers, 8 inches.
R. Peon. Red with white centre. Semi-double, 6 inches.
R. pumila. Pale pink, 18 inches.
R. Rouletti. Very double, pink, 6 inches.

SAPONARIA. Soapwort. An excellent plant for rock walls where it can be allowed to make large cushions. Light well drained soil in full sun. Easily raised from seed.

S. ocymoides. Masses of trailing stems. Covered with rose pink flowers in early summer, 6 inches.

SAXIFRAGA. No general instructions can be given for this family, as it comprises too many different types. They are divided into groups, and each requires slightly different treatment.

The Encrusted section include those with rosettes of tough leaves that are encrusted with white along the margins. These require open situations in very gritty soil, and do well in the upright crevices of large rocks. The flowers are generally arching sprays of white, or pale pinks and yellows.

S. cochlearis. Neat foliage. White flowers in May, 4 inches.

S. cotyledon (*pyramidalis*). Large-leaved rosette. Tall spires of pure white, 24 inches.

S. longifolia. Tumbling Waters. Long, narrow leaves. Plumes of white flowers, 15 inches.

The Mossy section require a leafy loam, and must have a certain amount of moisture during the summer. Similar treatment suits the Umbrosa types, which are the London Pride saxifrages.

S. decipiens. Very many named hybrids from pure white, through pink, to deepest red. Flowering in May and June, heights vary from 4–9 inches.

S. umbrosa. The familiar London Pride. Pink flowers in May and June, 12 inches.

S. primuloides Elliot's var. A smaller growing plant, very like the above. The flowers are a deeper pink, and they are only 6 inches high.

The Kabschia section are dwarf, cushion-forming plants.

They need well drained, gritty soil and a sunny position. They are the earliest of the saxifrages to flower in the spring, and have a large range of colours. The named hybrids are very numerous, and in many cases hard to distinguish one from the other. They are perfect plants for crevices in bare rock, and in this position avoid getting over-run with moss, which is one of the most difficult of " weeds " to remove, as it gets right through the whole cushion of leaves.

S. apiculata. Easily grown. Yellow. March, 3 inches.

S. a. alba. White flowered form of the above.

S. Arco-Valleyi. A very neat growing Hybrid with close, grey green leaves. Shell pink flowers on very short stems. A well grown specimen in the alpine house is a beautiful sight in March.

S. burseriana and its hybrids. Flowering from early in January, these are grand little plants with very large blooms on 2 inch stems.

S. b. crenata. White with the edges of the petals frilled.

S. b. gloria. Large, pure white flowers. The stems are reddish.

S. b. sulphurea. Flowers soft sulphur yellow.

S. Elizabethae. Dark green, spiny leaves. Flowers strong yellow. Easy to grow and forms large clumps in a few seasons.

S. Faldonside. Close cushions. Pale yellow flowers with red buds and stems. February, 2 inches.

S. Jenkinsii. One of the easiest of the close growing types. Pale pink flowers on 1 inch stems cover the whole plant.

S. Myra. Flat cushions of green. Deep pink flowers on very short stems in March. Very good in the scree.

S. Lady B. Stanley. Deep cerise flowers, 1 inch. Protect from the full glare of the sun in summer.

S. Kellereri. A beautiful plant with strong, silver green rosettes. Flowers are branching heads of pink very early in January, 3 inches.

S. sancta. Yellow, 3 inches. Rather like S. apiculata and Elizabethae.

Another small section called Porphyrions. These are prostrate, trailing plants that need a gritty, peat soil, and a position where it will not get too dry in summer.

S. oppositifolia. The flowers are red purple and practically stemless. Late February, 1 inch.

S. o. splendens. Flowers larger than the above.

S. o. W. A. Clarke. The petals are slightly pointed, giving the flowers a star-like appearance. Flowers purple crimson.

S. retusa. A miniature of the group. The flowers, which are tiny stars, are carried on branching stems 1 inch high.

The Engleria section are mid-way in appearance between the Kabschias and the Encrusteds, having flat rosettes of leaves that are broader than most of the Kabschias. Gritty soil and positions in full sun. The flowers are borne on stems a few inches high, generally curled over at the top. These stems are frequently covered with coloured hairs, which add to the general beauty of the plant.

S. Biasoletti. Silver rosette of leaves. The arched flower spikes are red.

S. Frederici-Augusti. Grey leaves edged with silver. Flowers pink with wine red buds.

S. Grisebachii. The most handsome of the section. Large rosettes of green leaves marked with silver. The flower spikes are 4 inches high, with reddish hairs, the petals pink and white. A large pan of this in the alpine house is a sight worth remembering.

There are other types that are not often used in the rock garden, so will not be mentioned here.

SCABIOSA. Need well drained soil in a sunny position. Can be increased by seed or division of plants.

S. graminifolia. Long, narrow, greyish leaves. Large, lavender flowers on wiry stems all through the summer, 9 inches.

S. Pterocephala. Prostrate hummock of rounded, grey leaves. Covered with pinkish lilac flowers on 1 inch stems. Looks well in paving or on a rocky bank.

SCUTELLARIA. Skull cap. Compact little plant for a sunny position on a rock wall. Light soil is needed where it will spread by underground shoots. Increase by division or cuttings.

S. japonica. Dark violet flowers in July, 6 inches.

SEDUM. Stonecrop. A large family of which only a collector would need more than a few. The naming is rather muddled as many of the species are very similar. They all have fleshy leaves and thrive in dry, sunny positions and light, sandy soil, though most of them will grow in any ordinary garden soil. Increase is no problem as the smallest bit will root in sand, and some varieties are too prolific with seed. They are invaluable for paving and walls, the varied colour of the leaves giving interest all the year round, as well as the large flower heads during the summer.

S. acre. A native stonecrop. Green leaves and golden flowers, 3 inches.

S. album. Another quick growing plant. White flowers, 3 inches.

S. Anacampseros. Trailing stems 6 inches long, ending in heads of purple flowers in July.

S. dasyphyllum. Mauvish grey leaves. White flowers, 1 inch.

S. ellacombianum. Bright yellow flowers, 6 inches.

S. glaucum. Pink flowers, 2 inches.

S. g. aureum. Golden leaves, pink flowers, 2 inches.

S. kamtschaticum. Upright growth. Heads of deep gold flowers, 6 inches.

S. lydium. The small, green leaves go red at the tips in poor soil and look doubly attractive. Flowers white, 3 inches.

S. middendorffianum. Upright growth. Golden flowers, 6 inches.

S. populifolium. A little tree sedum that loses its leaves in winter. Flowers white, 9 inches.

S. Sieboldii. Prostrate stems of grey leaves. Lovely pink flowers in August, 6 inches.

S. spathulifolium. Rather large leaves covered with a grey "bloom" like a ripe plum. Yellow flowers, 2 inches.

S. s. atropurpureum. The leaves are a rich red, otherwise like the above. Both excellent for paving, screes or the alpine house.

S. spurium. Very rampant and thrives even in semi-shade. Pale pink, starry flowers, 6 inches.

S. s. purpureum. The leaves have a reddish tinge. Flowers deep crimson, 6 inches.

SEMPERVIVUM. Houseleek. Another huge family of plants with fleshy leaves, and again with great confusion as to naming. They form large, round, fleshy rosettes of various shades. The flower spikes are generally large, and after flowering the rosette dies, but a ring of tiny offsets on runners carries on the life of the plant. They will grow almost anywhere—on the top of a bare wall with practically no soil, in a rock crevice or in paving; in fact, any place that the drainage is good; waterlogged soil is about the only thing that will kill them. Increased by division of the offsets or by seed.

S. arachnoideum. The Cobweb Houseleek. Small rosettes covered with a mass of fine hairs like spiders' webs. The plant should have a pane of glass over it in winter to protect it from rain, cold does not injure it. The flowers are large sprays of rosy pink, 6 inches.

S. calcareum. Large rosettes of reddish purple with a grey sheen. Looks very well planted with other species of different colours.

S. Comolli. General colour bronze, but some rosettes have red patches in the centre.

S. glaucum. Bright green rosettes.

S. montanum. Dark green rosettes.

S. ornatum. Very handsome rosettes of deep ruby red.

S. soboliferum. Hen and Chicken's Houseleek. Small, round rosettes of red and green. The offsets are produced in large numbers, like tiny marbles that sit on top of the old plants, later these roll off and start a new colony further down the slope.

SHORTIA. A woodland plant from Japan that needs a peat soil and a position in shade. Not easy to grow.

S. uniflora. Leathery leaves. Large bell-shaped flowers of soft rose pink in spring, 6 inches.

SILENE. Catchfly. They need light soil in a sunny position, and are easily increased from seed or cuttings.

S. acaulis. Neat cushions of glossy green leaves. Studded in summer with stemless, pink flowers. Very useful for providing green in the scree, as it tends to look very barren and stony in winter, 2 inches.

S. alpestris. White, starry flowers in May and June, 3 inches.

S. Schafta. Large tufts of flower stems that produce many rosy magenta flowers in summer and for several months, 6 inches. Excellent in the rock wall.

SISYRINCHIUM. Blue-eyed Grass. These look like miniature Irises, and have grassy leaves and starry flowers on the top of stiff stems. The petals close up at night. They grow in light soil in a sunny position and are easily increased by division.

S. angustifolium. Clear blue flowers with a deeper eye. Summer, 4 inches.

S. Bermudianum. Violet blue flowers, 9 inches.

S. californicum. Bright yellow flowers, 9 inches. Sets seed freely.

SOLDANELLA. Beautiful plants needing a damp soil of peat and coarse gravel. The flowers are hanging bells with fringed edges. Slugs are very fond of the flower buds, and will eat out the whole heart of the plant in the winter. Seed grows freely, but the tiny seedlings are awkward to handle, having very long, hairy roots making pricking out a fiddly job. Looks well grown in pans.

S. alpina. Round, leathery leaves. Violet blue, 3 inches. March and April.

S. montana. Like the above, but larger, 6 inches.

SOLIDAGO. Golden Rod. Only one dwarf variety will be mentioned. Grows in any good garden soil, and is a suitable companion for the dwarf Michaelmas daisies (Aster pygmaeus).

S. brachystachys. Bright yellow flowers. Autumn, 8 inches.

STATICE. Sea Lavender. Will grow in any well drained garden soil. The " everlasting " flowers are useful, flowering in August and remaining in good condition until the winter. Increase by seed.

S. bellidifolia. Small rosettes of tough, oval leaves. Sprays of mauve flowers, 6 inches.

S. incana. Large sprays of white flowers with pinkish mauve bracts and stems, 9 inches.

THYMUS. Thyme. A useful family of fragrant herbs, the creeping varieties being the perfect plants for clothing paving, as they do not resent a reasonable amount of traffic, and also give out their spicy smell when crushed underfoot. Light soil in full sun is needed. Most varieties are easily increased by division.

T. citriodorus Silver Queen. Lemon scented bush of variegated silver leaves. Flowers pale mauve in July, 9 inches.

T. Herba-barona. The Caraway scented thyme. Spreading growth and deep purple flowers. June, 4 inches.

T. serpyllum. A creeping variety for covering walls and paving. There are many forms of different colours. They start flowering in June and continue to give a display of colour until August, 1 inch.

T. s. Annie Hall. Green leaves. Flowers flesh pink.

T. s. carneus. Dark green leaves. Pink flowers.

T. s. coccineus. Deep reddish green leaves. Flowers crimson.

T. s. lanuginosus. Leaves covered with hairs which give a grey appearance. Flowers mauvish pink.

T. s. major. Leaves larger than the others. Flowers crimson, 2 inches.

TUNICA. Useful for seeding about among other plants, but should not be planted by itself, as the whole plant is too light and feathery to cover the ground. Any ordinary garden soil in a sunny position.

T. Saxifraga. Pale pink flowers on wiry stems from June till September. Looks like Gypsophila, 6 inches.

VERBENA. This plant is not hardy, but is included because it supplies a colour that is very scarce in the rock garden. Will spread quickly, rooting as it goes, in light soil in a sunny position. Cuttings root easily, and a few kept in a frame or house for the winter will ensure a supply for the next year. Watch out for greenfly, which are often troublesome on the young shoots.

V. chamædryfolia. Prostrate growth. Large, round flower heads of intense scarlet all through the summer.

VERONICA. Speedwell. A huge family of plants that includes shrubs, tall herbaceous plants and low spreading plants. Most of them will grow in ordinary garden soil and prefer sunny positions. Can be increased by cuttings, division and seed.

V. Bidwilli minor. Tiny little leaves on thread-like stems. Grow it for the foliage, and the small, white flowers will not be a disappointment, 2 inches. Does well in the scree or alpine house.

V. cinerea. Silver leaves. Spikes of blue flowers, 4 inches.

V. incana. Grey leaves. Spikes of deep blue flowers in July, 9 inches.

V. pectinata. Prostrate woolly leaves. Sprays of blue flowers in May and June.

V. p. rosea. Like the above with pink flowers.

V. repens. Shiny, green leaves that lie close to the

ground, the stems rooting as they go. White flowers in May, 1 inch.

V. spicata. Rather like V. incana, but with green leaves. There are pink, blue and white flowered forms.

V. Teucrium dubia, or **V. prostrata** or **V. rupestris—** they all seem to be the same plant. An excellent plant, easy to grow, that covers the ground with a mat of green leaves. Covered with three inch long " tails " of bright blue flowers in May.

VIOLA. These plants need good soil to do well and give a good show of flowers. Increased in various ways, according to variety.

V. biflora. A tiny, bright yellow Violet. Two flowers are produced on each 3 inch stem. Plant in a shaded position in leafy soil.

V. cornuta. Easily grown. Produces masses of slender, butterfly flowers in spring and summer. Flowers are white, shades of light blue and good purple. Many named varieties, some of which are rather large and should be used as bedding violas, they look too formal for the rock garden.

ZAUSCHNERIA. Californian Fuchsia. A grand plant for giving a display of orange in the autumn garden. Spreads freely by underground stems, if planted in good, light loam in a sunny position. Once settled, it will penetrate into narrow cracks in the rocks and thrive on very little soil. Increase by division, this is best done after growth has started in spring.

Z. californica. Spikes of tubular orange flowers in August and September, 12 inches.

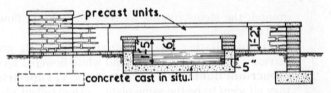

precast units.

1'·2"

·5"

6"

concrete cast in situ.

5"

CROSS SECTION.

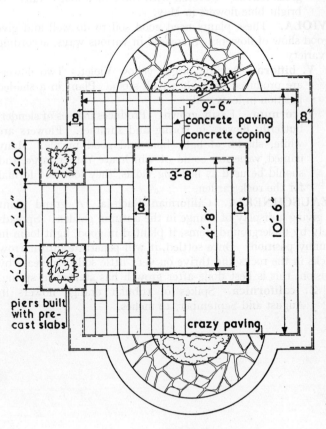

2'·3" rd.

9'-6"

concrete paving

concrete coping

8"

8"

3'-8"

8"

8"

4'-8"

10'-6"

2'-0"

2'-6"

2'-0"

**piers built
with pre-
cast slabs**

crazy paving

PLAN.
A CONCRETE GARDEN POOL.

CHAPTER XII

THE GARDEN POOL—ITS
CONSTRUCTION AND SURROUNDS

Do you know ? —

1. An informal pool " goes " with the rock garden.
2. Even a tub will do !
3. How to make a concrete pool.
4. " Season " the pond before you stock with fish.
5. What shall I put round the edge— ?

RIGHT the way throughout the ages people have felt the need of water in the garden. The Monasteries had their fish ponds so that the monks could easily collect their fish for Fridays. The Indian and Persian Gardens found water necessary for irrigation, and perhaps it really is to the East that we owe much of our love of a pool—for cool places are certainly appreciated by those who live in the warmer climes. There is a Persian motto referring to a pool which says : " If there is a Heaven upon earth—it is here—it is here."

The pool may be of value for the reflections it gives, and even in quite a small garden reflections can, of course, be arranged. There is always the biological reflection, the fish and the other water life, let alone the beauty and scent which can be got from Aquatic Plants.

The pool can either be formal or informal, and later on in the chapter we deal in fair detail with the various types. The formal pool would be made so as to be a centre piece perhaps, and so to form a special " garden " on its own. It is often quite suitably placed at the bottom of the lawn, or even quite near the house, as an adjunct to a paved pathway or court. If informal, it can be made close to the rock garden and will then be connected to it by a small stream. It may find itself situated in a particular part of the garden because of a natural depression there, also the pool may be excavated in such a manner that it certainly looks natural. Each garden has its own problems, but somewhere in most gardens there is room and possibly a need for a small or even a large water garden.

TUB CULTIVATION

Those who have too small a garden to make a pool of any kind, may sink a tub into the ground and use this. A good type for the purpose would be one which is 30 inches across and 18 inches deep. Never, of course, use a barrel which has contained soap, oil, petrol or paraffin, but on the other hand, old beer barrels and wine casks are excellent.

GROWING WATER LILIES IN A TUB

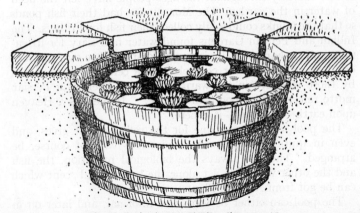

TUB SUNK IN THE GROUND.

Remember the barrel should be sunk 3 inches below ground level and some rocks arranged round so as to overhang. Suitable plants, such as the mimulus and primulas, can be planted around the edge, and if a little rock edge is made other plants, like spiræas and trollius and iris, may be planted also. Tubs such as have been described will accommodate about six goldfish, and say, six oxygenators, three aquatic plants, choosing those that throw their foliage and flowers well above water level, and a sprinkling of scavengers.

Nymphæa Pygmæa Helvola. A delightful
variety for shallow pools or tubs.

Nymphæa stellata, a beautiful tropical water
lily with scented flowers. One of the best
for tub cultivation.

THE ROUND " DISH-SHAPED " POOL

The most simple pool to make is the " dish-shaped " pool, which does not require any shuttering.

The ground is excavated, making the sides to a flat slope. In selecting the site, choose one that is on undisturbed soil and away from any trees, otherwise there is a likelihood of the pond cracking.

After the soil has been dug, it should be well rammed, and any soft places filled in with clinker or rubble to get a firm and even sub-base. This is essential, as it must be remembered that the " dish " rests on the earth, and if one part of the ground is much softer than another, the " dish " will tend to sink in the soft places and that may lead to cracks appearing.

When the preparation of the ground has been completed, a concrete composed of one part of cement and three parts of sand is used to line the surface. Its thickness should be at least 3 inches, and additional strength can be obtained if stout wire netting is placed in the centre of the concrete to act as reinforcement.

Another good tip, is to cover the soil with paper before placing the concrete. This will help to prevent the soil from absorbing the water from the concrete.

The pond can be made to any shape by this method, but its size should not exceed about 4 foot in diameter, and the depth should not be greater than 18 inches, otherwise difficulty will arise in placing the concrete in one operation.

With sloping ground and a series of small pools, a very delightful effect can be obtained. Another idea, is to dig a circular channel to form an island in the centre.

THE RECTANGULAR POOL

A very simple type of pool is one which is rectangular, and the great advantage of this type of pool, perhaps, is that a varying depth of water can be provided, one end being, say, 12 inches or so deeper than the other. It is usual also to provide a ledge about 12 inches wide and 4 inches below the

E

A RECTANGULAR POOL

water level

2'6" deep end.
1'6" shallow end.

6"

18"

normal water level so that if fish are kept, the fry will find a hiding place during the spawning season, where they will not be worried by other fish. Alternatively, the bottom of the pool can be stepped so as to provide a shallow area.

The thickness of the concrete depends on the depth of the water, but a thickness of at least 4 inches will be required for most ponds.

A typical design for a lily pool will be found in the illustration. It will be seen that the greatest depth is 2 feet 6 inches at one end, and that the bottom is sloped up to a depth of 1 foot 6 inches at the other end. The length and width will depend on the size of the garden.

SITE PREPARATION

When the position of the pool and the design have been decided upon, it is necessary to carry out soil excavation. The top soil should first be removed and the position of the pool marked out with pegs and string lines. The disposal of the excavated soil should not present a problem, as it can very often be used for making a raised bed around the pool to give it a sunken effect.

After the digging is completed, the bottom of the pool should be well rammed and levelled to provide a firm and even base for the concrete. In cases where the ground is soft, a 3 inch layer of broken bricks, rubble or similar dry material should be spread over the bottom and well rammed. This will tighten the soil and help to make a firm base.

CONSTRUCTION OF THE POOL

The next step is concreting the bottom of the pool, and whether it can be accomplished in one operation will largely depend on the size of the pool, and the facilities available for mixing the concrete. Timber pegs should be driven at intervals across the width and along the length of the pond, the tops of which should be level with the desired thickness of concrete.

An easy method for setting these pegs, is to fix one at each end of the pool at the correct level, and then by means of a tightened string attached to the end pegs, drive the other pegs in at suitable intervals until their tops are level with the string.

MIXING THE CONCRETE

The materials required for concrete are British Portland cement, sand, and shingle, and for pool work the concrete should be composed of one part of cement, two parts of sand, and three parts of shingle, graded from $\frac{3}{4}$ inch down to $\frac{3}{16}$ inch. In some localities, it may be found necessary to use crushed stone for the aggregate instead of shingle. This is quite satisfactory, provided the material does not contain any very fine dust. The cement, sand, and shingle should all be measured by volume in the same sized receptacle, so as to obtain the correct proportions. An ordinary bucket is quite suitable for this purpose.

It is after the cement and sand have been thoroughly mixed in their dry state that the shingle or broken stone is added, and the whole mix is then given a further turning before the water is added. The water should be added a little at a time while the materials are being turned over until a plastic and easily workable mix is obtained.

PLACING THE CONCRETE

Immediately before placing the concrete, the bottom of the excavation should be sprinkled with water, but no pools of water left. The concrete is then simply spread over the ground, using a stout piece of timber for tamping, until it is level with the top of the pegs. These pegs should be removed as the work progresses, and the top surface should be finished off with a wooden float.

The edges of the bottom slab on which the walls will rest, should be roughened in order to form a key between the sides and the bottom. This is important, as pools sometimes leak at this junction due to an imperfect joint.

Where it is not possible to complete the slab in a day, a straight piece of wood should be placed across the width of the pool and the concrete finished to this point.   To complete the slab, the timber is removed and the edge of the slab roughened. The loose pieces of concrete should be removed, and immediately before placing the new concrete, the roughened edge should be given a thick coat of cement grout, made by mixing equal parts of cement and sand with water to the consistency of thick oil paint.

After the slab has hardened sufficiently, it should be covered with damp sacks to prevent the concrete from drying out too quickly.

PLACING CONCRETE IN FROSTY WEATHER

It should be noted that concrete work should not be carried out when the temperature is below 35 degrees F. on a falling thermometer, but during mild weather conditions when the day temperatures are above 35 degrees F. and the night temperatures a few degrees below freezing point, concrete work may be carried out by using hot water for mixing.   The temperature of the water should be about 150 degrees F. Mixing is carried out in the usual manner, the cement, sand and stone being mixed first in their dry state before the water is added.

On no account should the hot water be added to the cement alone, and frozen aggregate should be thawed by pouring a few buckets of water (boiling) over the heap.

Experience shows that when water of the above temperature is added to the mix, the temperature of the concrete is raised to about 65 degrees F., i.e. summer temperature, thus providing sufficient heat for the chemical action involved in the setting and hardening of the cement to take place.

In order that the heat may be retained and the chemical action continued, all newly placed concrete should be covered at night with waterproof paper, straw, sacks, hessian or similar dry material which should be firmly held down in order to prevent it from becoming dislodged.   Sacks partly filled with straw and laid flat on the surface give excellent protection.

The protective covering should be kept in position until the

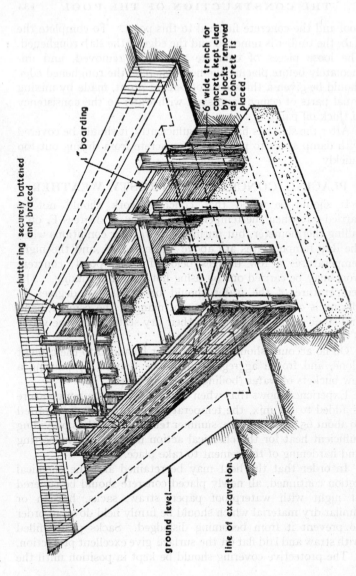

6" wide trench for concrete kept clear by blocks removed as concrete is placed

1" boarding

shuttering securely battened and braced

ground level

line of excavation

SHUTTERING IN PLACE FOR MAKING A POOL

concrete has hardened, but during the day, if the temperature is well above freezing point, the covering may be removed and the work cured in the usual manner.

Although the concrete made in winter time is slow in hardening, the desired result is eventually obtained, and no anxiety need be felt if it is found that the concrete remains soft for one or two days.

SHUTTERING

The timber framework for the walls of a rectangular pool does not call for a very great knowledge of carpentry, and can quite easily be constructed by the amateur. The framework generally consists of a bottomless box, securely battened and braced to prevent the timber from bulging during the placing of the concrete.

The drawing opposite shows the formwork for a pool, consisting of 1 inch boards battened together with 2 inch by 2 inch timbers, and securely braced so that it will be rigid. The formwork is made in panels, and erected in the pool. To prevent it from moving, the forms should be blocked on all sides against the earth. This is shown in the drawing, the blocks being removed as the wall concrete is placed.

In order to facilitate the removal of the forms, it is advisable to oil the surface against which the concrete will be placed. Proprietary brands of mould oil, specially made for the purpose, can be obtained or a mixture of 75 per cent. paraffin oil and 25 per cent. raw linseed oil may be used.

CONCRETING THE SIDES

The mix of concrete given for the bottom is also recommended for the walls. Concrete should be placed in even layers working gradually round the pool, and consolidated with a stout piece of timber.

If the walls cannot be completed in a day, then it will be necessary to form a horizontal construction joint. The concrete at this joint should be left fairly level and protected from the weather by covering the wall at the top of the formwork with waterproof paper or sacking.

Before proceeding with the concreting, roughen the surface, taking care to remove the broken pieces of concrete, and apply a thick coat of cement grout so that new concrete will form a proper bond with that already placed.

REMOVING THE SHUTTERING

The forms should be left in position for at least three days, and during that period the concrete should be kept wet. After the timbers have been removed, the pond may be filled with water, and the water level marked on the side in pencil.

During the first few days, it is usual to find a considerable drop in the water-level. This does not mean that the pool leaks, as a certain amount of water is absorbed by the concrete. Losses due to evaporation, which are quite considerable on a very hot day, also have to be considered.

THE ROUND, FLAT-BOTTOMED POOL

This is made in the same way as the rectangular pool, but the formwork may consist of a circular framework of timber to which is secured plywood or some other material which is easily bent to shape.

SEASONING

Before plants or fish are introduced, it is necessary to season the pool. The usual method is to fill the pool and leave it for a week or so, and after this period to scrub the sides vigorously with a hard brush. The pond should then be emptied and refilled. This process should be carried out two or three times before the pond is ready for stocking.

Another method, which has proved quite successful, is to paint the inside of the pool with a 1-in-4 solution of waterglass. This needs to be done two or three times at intervals of two or three days.

Whatever method is adopted, the greatest of care should be taken to see that the seasoning is perfect, and this can be done by introducing a few tadpoles or even small goldfish into the water. If they show no ill effects, then the pond is seasoned and so safe to be stocked with more expensive fish.

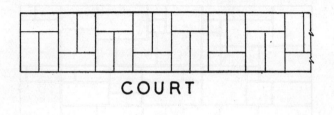

COURT

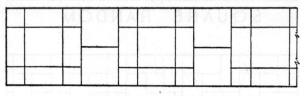

BLAGRAVE

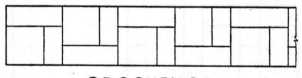

GROSVENOR

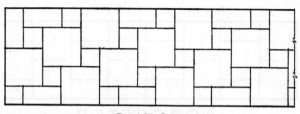

DUTCH

E*   SURROUNDS FOR A POOL

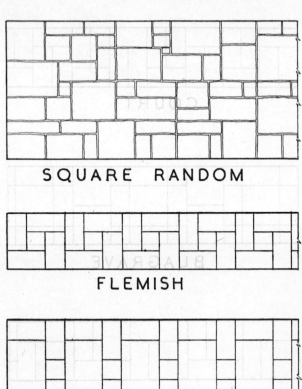

SQUARE RANDOM

FLEMISH

CHERITON

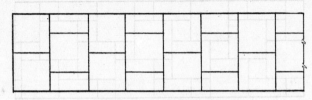

WORCESTER

SURROUNDS FOR A POOL

Another method is to paint the inside of the pool with a bituminous paint. Fortunately these paints can be obtained in colours, and their use enables the owner to provide the pool with a coloured finish. Another great advantage of a bituminous paint is that it is waterproof, and so the impermeability of the pool is increased. As a matter of fact, the blue and green bituminous paints look very attractive.

Or there is a proprietary product with which the work can be completed in four days (one application every day), and after a thorough rinse out the pool will be perfectly watertight and ready for filling. This product also possesses the property of instantly stopping the caustic action of fresh cement which is so injurious to fish and plant life.

Those with a scientific mind may care to use a solution of commercial phosphoric acid to neutralize the alkalinity of the water. The pool is filled with clean water, left for a day or two, and then a solution of commercial phosphoric acid is added until red litmus paper no longer turns blue. The pond is then emptied and refilled.

About a pound of commercial phosphoric acid is sufficient for the average small pond, this and the red litmus paper may be obtained quite cheaply from most chemists.

COPING

The coping stones to be used around the edge of the pond can be made with concrete slabs of any shape and size. The great advantage of using coping stones of some kind, is that they may be laid so that they project over the edge of the pool, and so hide any irregularities of the pool walls. It is quite easy to change the appearance of a rectangular pond to the shape of an informal pool if the slabs are laid irregularly around the edges.

THE POOL SURROUND

It is sometimes necessary to lay paving stones as a surround to the pool, and these may be made at home with cement and sand. By making various sizes of slabs, very attractive

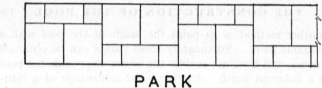

PARK

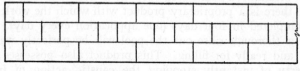

SNECKED LACED

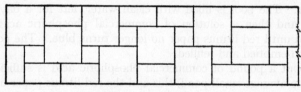

ACACIA

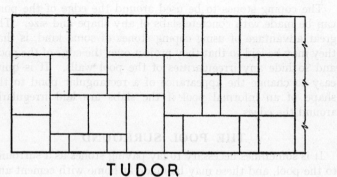

TUDOR

SURROUNDS FOR A POOL

patterns can be formed, as will be seen in the diagrams, on pages, 137, 138 and 140.

It is quite simple to lay the concrete in situ, and before it has hardened to cut double lines into the surface, $\frac{3}{8}$ inch apart and about $\frac{1}{2}$ inch deep, to conform to the pattern it is desired to reproduce. These lines form the joint lines, and when the concrete has hardened, the concrete between these lines may be removed to give the appearance of paving.

OXYGENATORS

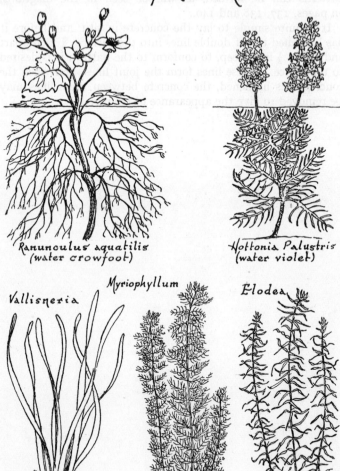

Ranunculus aquatilis
(water crowfoot)

Hottonia Palustris
(water violet)

Vallisneria

Myriophyllum

Elodea

CHAPTER XIII

BALANCE AND PREPARATION

Do please—
1. Keep the water " sweet."
2. Do not worry when the water turns misty.
3. Have the correct balance.
4. Ask water snails to help.

IF the pool is to be a success and is not going to be " smelly " or prove a breeding place for insects, it will be necessary to put in plants of various kinds. There is a very wide choice of plants, very fortunately. There are floating Aquatics, Oxygenators, Ordinary Aquatics, Ferns, Rushes and tall growing perennials for the surrounds. These, with the fish, and the crustacea will help to keep the water sweet.

CONTROLLING ALGAE

Soon after the pool has been stocked with plants and fish, it will be found that the clarity of the new water disappears. The owner of the pool will be distressed, and will immediately consider emptying the pool and refilling, but this should not be done, as the clouding is part of a natural cycle. The water will turn opaque, and subsequently become green. The opaqueness will be due to chemical changes in the soil, either used in the bottom of the pool or in the pots that are submerged, and the greenness is due to algae (microscopic plants).

Providing the pool has been properly stocked with the correct plants and live stock to give the necessary balance, in a few months the water should again become perfectly clear. Sometimes this may take as long as eighteen months.

Algae in themselves, providing they do not get too numerous, do no harm to the fish, but rather will they benefit them. Algae are great oxygenators. Where algae growth is excessive it will exhaust the water constituents upon which it is sustained, and so ultimately it will diminish to normal proportions. It is in the newly-built pond that the propaga-tion of the algae is very rapid, and it is always worse in a pool exposed to strong sunlight.

One kind of algae is known as Blanket Weed, and this may prove troublesome. It makes excessive and dense growth and may strangle other aquatic plants and even harm small fishes. This weed is too often introduced accidentally when planting aquatic plants which have been obtained from pools in the country. The long, hair-like green threads combine into a solid mat which justifies the name blanket weed.

If excessive growth of this weed does appear, it is necessary to remove pond life, and then to sterilize the pool with permanganate of potash. This is done by placing a handful of crystals in a muslin bag, attaching this to the end of a stick or piece of string, and then swirling it about in the water until it has changed to a rich purple colour. After a day's soaking, the pool may be emptied and replenished with fresh water, care of course, being taken to see that the great majority of the solution is removed.

Another method of control, is by the use of powdered copper sulphate, but very little copper sulphate is necessary. If the minutest quantities are used then the goldfish are not harmed, and it has been suggested that all that is required is an amount equal to $\frac{1}{8}$ ounce per 1,000 gallons. Such a dose may be applied at one-monthly intervals if necessary, during the spring and autumn.

Other methods of helping to control the growth of algae are : (1) To plant marginal plants or bushes on the sunny side of the water so as to give shade. (2) To introduce water lilies or other floating aquatics, and (3) to stock the pond with various crustacea, such as water fleas, cyclops and aquatic snails.

BALANCE

It should be remembered that the waste matter which accumulates in the pool is considerable, and this makes it essential that sufficient plants are grown to absorb all this material. As a general guide, I should say that one plant is necessary to every square foot, or at any rate, every two square feet, but this includes the smaller growing subjects as well as the larger ones. The more sparsely the pool is planted, the longer it takes to mature.

It may be necessary to layer the pond with soil and to plant the various aquatics that need it in this. A heavy fibrous meadow loam is excellent for the purpose, and it is always better to avoid sand, leaf-mould and peat or the soil from ponds or rivers. The loam should be spread on the bottom of the pool to the depth of 6 or 7 inches and it should be slightly moistened and then well rammed.

It is possible to furnish the pool with plants grown in pots, and these may either be stood on shelving, made specially for the purpose, or on temporary stands dropped into the pool.

Where water lilies are to be grown, it may be possible to place twelve months old, well-decayed cow manure in the bottom of the pool first of all, and then to put the soil on top. Quite a good substitute is a coarse bonemeal, and a sixteenth of an inch dusting all over the bottom of the pool should be sufficient.

There is a common belief that it is necessary to cover the soil with sand or shingle, and that this will help to keep the water clear. There is no need to do this, for the use of shingle has got nothing to do with the clearness, but this, as has already been stated, will be brought about if there is a correct balance of plants, fish and snails.

CHAPTER XIV

WATER LILIES

I want to tell you that—

1. Water lilies need sun.
2. Hardy lilies don't mind frost.
3. Aquatics need different depths.
4. You must plant a selection.
5. You must study and try.

To be successful with water lilies they should have a full sunny position, or at any rate, a position where the sun reaches them from midday until the late afternoon. Water lilies should be planted after the middle of April, and during the months of May and June, just after the plants have started growing vigorously.

The roots of many of the species are extremely retentive of life, and I have known them be out of water for many months without losing vitality. The majority of water lilies open their flowers during the day and close them during the late afternoon, but some of the tropical forms seem to wait until the cool of the evening before they bloom and start to scent the air. Some lilies hold themselves erect out of the water as if reaching upwards for the sun; most, however, float on the surface of the pool and gently move as the breezes disturb the shimmering smoothness of the water. It is a curious thing that we get our water lilies from almost every country in the world except New Zealand.

The plants are lifted by severing nearly all the roots. These should never be confused with the root stock or the hard, fleshy part. Old roots would never take fresh hold anyway, and the plant soon grows out new roots directly it is transplanted. Some varieties have roots like bananas; others are like the base of celery; others are said to be like small potatoes or even nuts. The banana-like roots should be planted horizontally, the root being covered with one inch of soil and the crown left just exposed. Those with celery-like roots should have a hole of sufficient size made for them, so as to enable the plant to be set upright with the shortened roots pointing downwards and the crown just exposed. Those with potato- or nut-like roots may be planted in a similar manner to the first group.

In every case firm planting is necessary. Pressure should be applied around the root, but not so much pressure given that the fragile parts are damaged.

The observant man will notice from the soil mark, or from the growth or shape, how the water lily has been previously planted, and he can then imitate this as nearly as possible.

In order to prevent the plant from rising at all while the water is running into the pool, large stones may be placed around it and these can be left in position for, say, six weeks. After this time the new roots should have developed.

Various other methods of planting have been devised. (1) The planting of the water lily in a basket of compost, the crown being wedged into place by a series of turves cut to shape. These prevent the soil from escaping when the basket is lowered into position. (2) Instead of small baskets, shallow perforated aquatic pans may be used. These are specially made for the purpose and can be planted up in a similar manner to the baskets.

It is always best to cover the plants with only a few inches of water until growth commences, and then as the plants progress, the pool may be filled. Shallow water gets warm more quickly, and it is this warmth that encourages early growth.

Sometimes the plants have to be dropped into position after the pools have been filled, and in this case it is better to place the pans or baskets on to some temporary shelving made with bricks, and then as the plants progress, to lower them gradually.

If the hardy species of water lilies are grown, they can withstand all the frost that we experience in this country. The pool should be kept filled during the winter so that there is at least 10 inches of water covering the crown.

It is advisable when the pool is frozen, to break the ice from time to time, and this helps to keep the fish supplied with air. Some people prefer to cover the pool, or part of the pool with boards or sacking, so as to prevent the water from freezing underneath.

In the spring, when the water lilies are just bursting into growth, all the rubbish and the dead leaves which may have accumulated during the winter months can be cleared away. It is sometimes a good thing to drain the pool, and then to remove 2 inches or 3 inches of mud for, say, 1 inch round the crown of the water lily and to replace this with good fresh soil.

PESTS

MOSQUITO LARVAE. This pest appears early in summer, attacking both the leaves and the buds. The leaves turn yellow and the buds fail to mature. It is a very serious pest with young plants.

Control. Stock the pond with surface eating fish, such as golden carp, rudd and gold or silver orfe.

BLACK FLY. These aphides attack the flowers and the leaves during dry, sunny weather. The plants look most unsightly and the sucking of the sap may mar the perfection of the blooms.

Control. Spray with water by means of a hose or a syringe and so wash the aphides into the pool, where they will be devoured by the fish.

In very bad cases, paraffin emulsion may be used, the formula being $\frac{1}{2}$ ounce of soft soap (or a substitute "spreader"), 1 quart of boiling water to which is added $\frac{1}{2}$ pint of paraffin. This should be mixed together well by constant stirring and beating (it is better to keep the mixture hot while stirring is going on), and then should be added to 5 gallons of cold water. The final mixture may be sprayed on to the plants. Fish seldom suffer any harmful effect from such spraying.

ACCENTROPUS NIVEUS. If a silvery white butterfly is seen fluttering over the pool during a summer evening, then an attack of the Accentropus may be feared. The larva of this butterfly cuts irregular, circular holes in the leaves of the water lilies and then joins these together into a little " cubby hole " where it may pupate.

Control. Stock the pool with fish as suggested for the mosquito larva.

A LIST OF VARIETIES OF WATER LILIES

There are many more varieties of Water Lilies than people realize. The types range from white and pinks, to reds, crimsons and yellows. Then there are the singles and doubles, the highly scented kinds, and those with round, cup-like flowers or with star-shaped flowers.

For water over 3 feet deep, only the most vigorous kinds can be grown, and these are the varieties that should be grown in baskets. They should be planted temporarily in shallow water before being finally plunged in their permanent home.

The varieties have been classified into four groups, according to the depth at which they are best planted, and the area of the water they cover.

- (a) Plant in 6–12 inches of water, and may cover an area of 24 inches.
- (b) Plant in 1 foot of water, and may cover an area of 4 feet.
- (c) Plant in 2 feet of water, and may cover an area of 7 feet.
- (d) Plant in 3 feet of water, and may cover an area of 10 feet.

GROUP A

GRAZIELLA. The colour of the flowers changes from coppery red to orange yellow. Orange stamens. The flower is medium size. The foliage is pale green, mottled with distinct maroon. This variety is a good one for small pools.

LAYDECKERI.

    L. fulgens. The medium flowers are bright carmine to amaranth. The foliage is olive green with brown red

SOME FAVOURITE WATER LILIES
THREE TYPICAL "VARIETIES" NAMED BELOW

Gladstoniana

James Brydon

Rose Arey

spots. Flowers very freely and is good for small pools. Sweet scent.

L. lilacea. The colour changes from pink and white, to pink and crimson. The blooms are medium in size, scented, and free-flowering.

L. purpurata. Medium sized flowers, star-shaped, are wine red then crimson. Orange red stamens.

ODORATA.

O. minor. Small, star-shaped flowers of white with yellow anthers. The foliage is pale green and the leaves are small. Very fine scent, and a good choice for a pool.

PINK OPAL. Medium sized, star-shaped flowers of a pretty shade of deep coral pink. The flowers stand well out of the water and can be used for cutting purposes.

TETRAGONA.

T. helvosa. Attractive olive green foliage, heavily mottled maroon. A profusion of small, star-shaped, rich sulphur yellow flowers.

T. pygmaea alba. This is one of the smallest and daintiest of the water lilies. It has light green foliage, rounded, and tiny, star-shaped, snow white flowers. Could be grown in a receptacle 12–15 inches across and holding only 6–9 inches of water.

GROUP B

ALBATROSS. Large, star-shaped flowers, snow white, conspicuous golden yellow anthers; young foliage is dark purple changing to dark green.

CAROLINIANA.

C. perfecta. Large, open star-shaped flowers of salmon-flesh and sweetly scented.

COMACHE. Medium flowers change from apricot to deep red but the outer petals remain yellow. The foliage is pale green. This variety is tropical in appearance.

CONQUEROR. Very large flowers, brilliant red stained and spotted white. Scarlet stamens.

ELLISIANA. Medium sized flowers of vermilion red. The sepals are white, stained rose. Orange stamens. Olive green foliage.

FIRECREST. The flowers, medium size, are rich rose pink with brilliant orange stamens tipped fiery red, and are produced in great profusion.

FROEBELI. An old variety, scented. The flowers are medium, very rich wine colour and the foliage dark green with large leaves.

ODORATA. White flowers, medium, cup-shaped, scented. They open in early June and go on to October.

> **O. sulphurea** (*Odorata mexicana*). Dark olive green foliage, heavily mottled reddish brown. Soft sulphur yellow flowers.

> **O. Turicensis.** Medium sized, free flowering, rose pink. Delicious scent.

PAUL HARIOT. The flowers are medium, round and free. The colours change from copper pink (inside petals yellow pink) to bright red. The foliage is green with maroon spots.

ROSE AREY. Large, star-shaped flowers with slightly incurved petals. A uniform shade of deep rose pink, with orange stamens tipped yellow. The foliage is purple changing to green with age.

SANGUINEA. Brilliant crimson carmine flowers with orange red stamens. Large, green leaves spotted maroon.

SIOUX. On first opening, the flowers are chrome yellow, suffused bronze then going reddish orange copper. Olive green foliage. This is an unusual variety because of the colour changes.

SOMPTUOSA. Very large flower, rose pink spotted white. Inner petals deep rose, outer petals rose stained green. Deep orange stamens. Lovely scent.

SUNRISE. Pale yellow going deeper yellow. Large, pointed petals.

GROUP C

AMABILIS. The large, star-shaped flowers are salmon shaded white, to rose and deep pink in centre. The foliage is reddish, going green later.

BRACKLEYI.

   B. rosea (*Tuberosa odorata rosea*). Medium sized cup-shaped flowers are a glistening rose pink, standing well above the water. Delightful scent.

ESCARBOUCLE. Bright crimson flowers with matching stamens, and large. The foliage is green. The flowers are very free and lasting. This variety could also be in Group B.

FLAVA. Star-shaped flowers standing well above the water. Canary yellow with outer petals stained red. A shy bloomer.

FORMOSA. Large, open flowers with rounded petals. Soft rose turning deeper rose. Blush white sepals, rich golden yellow stamens, and pale green foliage.

GONNERE. Large, double, snow white flowers, the outer petals stained and striped green. Yellow stamens. Free flowering and lasts a long time.

HERMIONE. The star-shaped flowers are borne on stiff stems standing well above the surface of the water. Snow white with outer sepals stained green.

INDIANA. Flowers medium to large, yellowish orange changing through bronze orange to coppery red. Deep green foliage spotted maroon. A distinctive variety.

JAMES BRYDON. Paeony-shaped flower, crimson pink, with golden stamens. The young leaves are purple going green with age. Needs plenty of room.

MARLIACEA.

   M. carnea. The flowers are blush white stained rose towards the base of the petals. When transplanted, the flowers are usually pure white the first year. A strong growing variety with large flowers.

   M. chromatella. Large flowers of glistening yellow, over 7 inches in diameter. Dark green foliage mottled reddish brown.

MASANIELLO. Very large, paeony-like flowers, carmine rose minutely spotted carmine. Deep yellow stamens. The flowers stand several inches out of the water.

MOOREI. Soft canary yellow flowers, no conspicuous markings on the foliage. Similar to M. chromatella.

MRS. RICHMOND. Light green foliage. Huge flowers pale rose pink, growing darker with age, flushed white. Sepals white, golden yellow stamens.

GROUP D

ATTRACTION. Bright purplish crimson, slightly flaked white. Deep mahogany. Very large flowers. The foliage is first green purple then olive green.

COL. A. J. WELCH. Bright yellow, large, star-shaped flowers borne on stems 6 inches long. Very free flowering. Pale green foliage.

COLOSSEA. Very pale pink, going white. Large flowers. Large, dark green leaves. Flowers from May to October.

GLADSTONIANA (*Tuberosa alba*). Pure white paeony-like flowers. Green shading in the sepals. Needs so much room that it should only be grown in lakes and ponds.

TUBEROSA.

> **T. maxima.** Very vigorous variety with shell-shaped petals. Snow white. Can be grown in 3–4 feet of water. When planted in shallow water, the flowers stand 6–9 inches out of the water.

> **T. m. Richardsoni.** Globular, white flowers with pea green sepals. Yellow stamens. The first variety in bloom and continues till September. Needs a lot of room.

> **T. m. rosea.** Bright green foliage, flowers a soft pink shaded white. Fragrant.

VIRGINALE. Very large flowers with shell-shaped petals, snow white and rose at base. Golden yellow stamens. Flowers from May till September.

CHAPTER XV

AQUATIC PLANTS

A mixed bag here !

1. Aquatics provide shade for fish.
2. Plants do give " air."
3. Hardy orchids to grow round the pool.
4. Bog plants are fascinating.
5. What are floaters ?

In addition to the water lilies, there are a large number of miscellaneous aquatics which can be grown in the pool. Some will be used to break straight lines and clothe the rough edges. Most will help to create more natural effects, and all will help in the general build up of the pool as described in chapter twelve. Some will be grown in a more central position of the pool and some will be grown close to the margin. Care must be taken with the plants that have a creeping habit, as if these are not kept under control, they may well smother other specimens. If it is necessary to put in a plant of this kind, see that its roots are constricted in a concrete box or pan, or that they are planted in a kind of pocket out of which they cannot escape.

Ordinary aquatics may be planted very much in the same way as the water lily and in similar heavy, fibrous loam. The loam should be moistened before being introduced into the pool, and when in position, should be pressed down firmly. The chosen aquatics are then planted in the moist soil, and the pool filled with water.

Some plants need their crowns covered with 4 inches or 5 inches of water, others with 12 inches or 15 inches, and some even with only 2 inches or 3 inches. Some plants like their flowers and foliage floating above the surface, some have their foliage and flowers standing well above the water level, and so it has been deemed necessary to divide the varieties up into seven groups.

(1) Crown covered with 3 inches to 5 inches of water, foliage under water, flowers floating on or above water.

(2) Crown covered with 3 inches to 5 inches of water, foliage above water, flowers above water.

(3) Crown covered with 12 inches to 15 inches of water, foliage floating on surface, and flowers floating on surface.

(4) Crown covered with 3 inches to 5 inches of water, foliage floating on surface, flowers floating on surface.

(5) Crown covered with 2 inches to 4 inches of water.

(6) Crown covered with 12 inches to 15 inches of water, foliage well above water level, flowers well above water level.

(7) Floating, requiring no soil, grow outside in summer, must be wintered in warm house.

N.B. Details of all the plants seen in the list that follows will be found on pages 182 to 204.

AQUATIC PLANTS

The classification is according to the depth of the pool, and the way in which the plants grow, in, under or over the water.

1. Depth of water 3–5 inches. Flowers and foliage above the water.

Acorus Calamus
Alisma plantago-aquatica
A. natans (Flowers and foliage are floating).
Anthemis
Brazenia (Flowers and foliage are floating).
Butomus
Calla
Caltha
Cyperus
Dracocephalum
Eriophorum
Glyceria
Houttuynia
Hydrocotyle
Hypericum
Iris laevigata
I. pseudacorus
Juncus
Jussieua
Lycopus

Lysimachia
Mentha aquatica
Menyanthes
Mimulus luteus
Miscanthus
Myosotis
Nesæa
Orontium
Oxalis (Flowers and foliage are floating).
Peltandra
Phragmites
Ranunculus aquatilis
R. delfinifolius
Rorippa
Rumex
Sagittaria
Saururus
Scirpus
Typha
Zizania

2. Depth of water 12—15 inches.

Aponogeton (Flowers and foliage float).
Hippuris (Flowers and foliage are well above the surface).
Hydrocleis (Flowers and foliage float).
Limnanthemum (Flowers and foliage float).
Polygonum amphibium (Flowers and foliage float).
Ranunculus lingua var. grandiflora (Flowers and foliage are above the surface).
Sparganium (Flowers and foliage are above the water).
Villarsia (Flowers and foliage float).

3. Submerged Aquatics.

These are those plants whose flowers and foliage are borne under the surface of the water.

Apium	**Myriophyllum**
Callitriche	**Najas**
Ceratophyllum	**Œnanthe**
Elodea	**Potemogeton**
Ericaulon	**Ranunculus**
Fontinalis	**Rorippa**
Hottonia (not hardy)	**Sagittaria**
Litorella	**Utricularia**
Mayacea	

SUBMERGED OXYGENATORS

The submerged oxygenating aquatic plants are most essential to every pool. They absorb the carbon dioxide and retain the carbon for their own growth, returning the oxygen to the water. Some plants carry on this work better than others, and the list given contains the best of these. Bubbles of pure oxygen can often be seen coming out from the leaves of such plants under the influence of sunlight. If they are kept healthy, such plants will work every day to keep the water clear, and make unnecessary for the pool owner to empty and clean the pool as frequently as he would normally have to do.

Submerged aquatics provide the necessary shelter and shade for young fish and are suitable " homes " for the deposition of the spawn. Fish are always cannibalistic, but the babies can dart amongst the submerged plants and so elude the older fish, until they are large enough to fight for themselves. Many of these submerged plants are also a necessary source of food for fish, and provide them with the mineral salts they require.

Three plants that fish are particularly fond of are the common watercress, the elodeas and the callitriche. Care should be taken never to introduce duckweed and azolla into a pool, for both of them will spread too rapidly, and so will cover the surface of the pool with green leaves and rob it of its powers of reflection.

Lists of submerged oxygenating aquatics are now given.

A LIST OF OXYGENATING AQUATICS FOR WATER GARDENS

They are marked according to whether they grow outside only, or in indoor aquaria. Some species do well in either case.

(*) Denotes OUTSIDE.   (†) Denotes INDOOR.

* Apium nudiflorum
* † A. inundatum
* Callitriche autumnalis
* † C. aquatica
* † Ceratophyllum demersum
* † Elodea callitrichoides
* E. crispa
* E. densa
* † Eriocaulon septangulare
* † Hottonia palustris
* Myriophyllum spicatum
* Najas microdon
* Œnanthe fistulosa
* † Potomogeton crispus
* P. lucens
* P. pectinatus
* † P. pulsillus
* † Ranunculus aquatilis
* Rorippa
* Sagittaria natans
* S. subulata
* † Utricularia vulgaris

For detailed descriptions of these plants turn to pages 182 to 204.

FLOATING AQUATICS

Some aquatics float on the surface of the water and will grow in the water either with or without soil. Most of them grow masses of attractive foliage, and so provide shade and food for the fish, and incidentally for any other inhabitants there may be in the pool. Some floating aquatics are not hardy, and have to be taken into a warm greenhouse during the winter. Others, on the other hand, are perfectly hardy, and it is these that are listed below.

The flowers and foliage of this group are borne on or under the surface, but do not root into the soil.

> **Azolla**
> **Eichhornea** (not hardy)
> **Hydrocharis morsus-ranæ**
> **Lemna**
> **Riccia**
> **Stratiotes aloides**

As usual, the descriptions of these plants will be found in the lists given on pages 182 to 204.

HARDY ORCHIDS

Most people seem to have an idea that orchids are hot-house flowers, and that it is impossible to grow them in the garden. Actually, there are many hardy varieties which will grow quite well around the pool. Most of them like the moist situation and will grow well in a compost consisting of equal parts of good soil and rotted leaf-mould. In addition, the surface of the soil should be covered with living sphagnum moss. The following plants are perhaps the pick of the hardy varieties :

> **Calopogon pulchellus**
> **Cephalanthera rubra**
> **Cypripedium acaule** (Ladies' Slipper)
> **C. spectabile**
> **Epipactis gigantea**
> **E. palustris**
> **Habenaria psycodes** (Hinged Orchis)
> **Orchis foliosa**
> **O. latifolia**

The description of these plants will be found in the lists given on pages 182 to 204.

INSECTIVOROUS BOG PLANTS

These insect " eating " plants are most fascinating and may be planted around the edge of a pool in a compost consisting of peat and chopped sphagnum moss. Unfortunately, many of them are only half-hardy, and so have to be taken into the greenhouse for the winter. Some, like the sarracenia, are best planted in full sun and are quite hardy if grown in any wet, boggy situation. Details, however, of the various plants are given in the lists on pages 182 to 204.

Dionaea muscipula (Venus' Fly Trap)
Drosera rotundifolia (Sundew)
Sarracenia purpurea (Huntsman's Cup)

Gentiana
septemfida is one
of the earliest
gentians to grow
and can be relied
on to produce
a lovely splash
of colour.

Primula denticulata will grow well in the
damper portions of the rock garden.

CHAPTER XVI

FISH AND SCAVENGERS

We pass on to the problems—
1. Fish help the balance.
2. Don't have too many !
3. What kinds of fish ?
4. Some scavengers !
5. What are scavengers ?

No one would consider having a pool without its complement of hardy fish. Fishes do help also to ensure the correct balance of nature, and are most attractive when swimming about in the clear water. It is possible to keep many different varieties of fish, all of which will live together in peace and good will, in fact, the beauties of the different fish are set off one by another. It is a great mistake, on the other hand, to attempt to have too many fish, and the best way of estimating the number is to realize that it is only possible to have 1 inch of fish (that is leaving out the tail) to every gallon of water. It is much better to have fewer fish, and for them all to be healthy and fit, rather than to have large numbers of fish, many of which will die or will suffer badly.

As the fish get older their body bulk, that is their width and depth, naturally increases disproportionately to their length, and so this rule of 1 inch of fish per gallon does not hold good. It is always as well, therefore, to understock a pool so as to allow for increase in weight, and there is always the chance that youngsters will come along to increase the numbers. Healthy fish should always have the opportunity of swimming a length of eight times their length, that is to say, if a fish is 3 inches long, the pool should be at least 24 inches long. Fortunately, in the garden pool there is little trouble in this direction, and as the surface area of the pool is usually large, then there is an increased oxygenating power which allows for the increase in the size of the fish, as a rule.

It has already been said that all kinds of fish can be introduced, but if it is intended to have different kinds, the fish when put into the water should all be of approximately the same size. Just like boys at school, the large ones have a tendency to bully the small ones. Such bullying usually leads to the smaller fish being starved.

It is always better to purchase fish for a pool that have been living in a pool, rather than to get hold of fish that have been brought up in a large lake or in a running stream. Such fish may be diseased or may be covered with fish lice. The fishes taken from the rivers and streams will not like garden pool conditions, where there is no water movement.

FEEDING

When the fish have been first introduced, the beginner always tends to over-feed, and it is only when the hobby loses its novelty that the fish are in danger of starving. The actual danger of over-feeding is not that the fish will get too fat, but that the uneaten food will go bad and so encourage the growth of fungi.

Fishes eat much less in the winter than in the summer, for in their natural habitat food is scarcer at this time of the year. For the same reason, fish are more sluggish in the winter than in the summer. It is only necessary during the winter months to give a pinch of fish food on a sunny day, and if it is found that this food is eaten readily, then a little more might be given. In the summer they should be fed regularly just like any other domestic " animal ". The wise pool owner will feed the fish at regular times of the day, a good time being early in the evening. Regular feeding leads to tameness, and the fish will collect at the side of the pool at feeding time in a fascinating manner.

Do not be tempted just to throw the food in one mass at one point, or otherwise the fish will not get the exercise they ought to have in chasing after their meal. Be sure to scatter the food over as big an area as possible. This even distribution allows the smaller fish to " get a look in ".

It is quite a good plan to scald all dried food or to allow it to soak thoroughly before use. It then swells before being eaten, and so prevents indigestion and constipation. This scheme is not really necessary with the hardy types of fish, but is desirable where any fancy breeds are kept. The Celestials, the Fantails and the Telescopes for instance, as well as others of the same type, have bodies with abnormal internal organs and it is these that can easily become ill if fed with dried food.

Some fish are carnivorous, and they must have a diet of live food, typical examples are the Dog Fish, Cat Fish, and various types of the Bass family. Most other fish are omnivorous and so require animal food and vegetable food. This may be provided by some of the proprietary fish foods, like Perry's or Spratt's, which are easy to purchase. In addition to the proprietary brands, it is quite a good plan, once a month or so, to give a little powdered vermicelli, or a small handful of some cereal.

It is always wise to stock the pool with water fleas and lice, because these are rich in protein and will keep the fishes supplied with food during holiday periods. In addition, small, red worms may be given, maggots and fresh ant eggs. The dried ant eggs so often sold are of little value, for the husks are soon passed back by the fish, and so provide media for fungus growth. It should only be necessary to give the living food, i.e. the blood worms and the daphnia, once every three weeks or so, and then only during, say, the warmest nine months of the year.

A LIST OF SUITABLE FISHES FOR THE POOL

While, for the most part, the names given are those of hardy species, i.e. able to remain in the pool all the year, some half-hardy ones are mentioned because of their striking appearance. They need at least to spend the winter in an indoor aquarium with a minimum water temperature of 65 degrees F. This is particularly true of fancy Goldfishes, i.e. Veiltails, Telescopes, and Celestials.

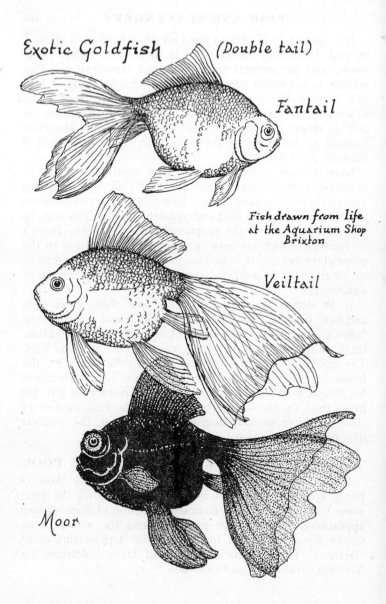

Exotic Goldfish (Double tail)

Fantail

Fish drawn from life
at the Aquarium Shop
Brixton

Veiltail

Moor

When buying Goldfish or any livestock for the pool, always go to a reputable English breeder. The author would be glad to recommend good firms. The reason for this is that the breeder's stock will have been reared and acclimatized to the vagaries of the British climate, whereas if fishes are purchased from abroad where they have been reared in warm water and intensively fed, they are less likely to survive in cold water.

Goldfish and certain other cold-water fishes of foreign origin may be purchased at any time of the year, but British cold-water fishes may not be bought or sold between March 15 and June 15 inclusive, as it is illegal to do so.

Do not buy undersized fish as they suffer more from changes of temperature than their bigger brothers. This is particularly true in Northern conditions.

See that the fish has a symmetrical body, look for bright eyes, liveliness, well spread fins, and see that there is no depression behind the gill plates. This can be seen when looking at the fish from above. There should also be no depression on the lower side of the body near the anus.

Goldfish (*Carassius auratus*).

These come in a variety of lovely colours, from pale yellow to pearly pink, red, and black.

Comet. A graceful fish with a long body, fins and tail. It looks " streamlined " especially as it is an active fish, always on the move. It is very hardy and accustomed to wintering outside.

Fantail. This has a thicker, stumpier body and a three-fold fan-like tail.

Primrose Fish. As intensely buttercup gold as some specimens are red.

Nymph. A sport from Veiltails, and has similar body and fins, but the tail is straight and may or may not be forked.

Shubunkin. A Goldfish with transparent scales, usually sprinkled and mottled with red, brown, yellow, white, and black. All these colours may not be on the same individual, but may be developed later. An attractive fish for the pool and aquarium.

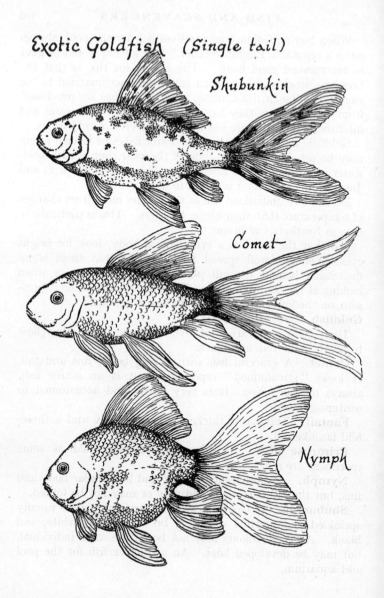

Exotic Goldfish (Single tail)

Shubunkin

Comet

Nymph

* **Telescope.** This fish has exceptionally protruding eyes.

* **Celestial.** This is similar to the Telescope, only its eyes point upwards instead of sideways.

* **Veiltail.** Their bodies are similar to the Fantail, but deeper. The fins and tails are more exaggerated, to such an extent that the former droops and the latter hangs down like a long skirt.

The species marked * are half-hardy and should be in water of at least 65 degrees F., especially in the winter. They are happiest in an indoor aquarium all the year.

Other Foreign Fish.

Bitterling. This is a very small carp and is sometimes known as the " Rainbow Fish " because of its lovely colours.

o **Catfish.** Very hardy and used to tank life. It should not be in the same pond as smaller fish, as it is pugnacious by nature.

Dogfish. A very hardy little fish, prettily marked in brown. Unlike other fish, it moves its fins alternately.

Golden Orfe. This is gradually proving more popular than the Goldfish, on account of its hardiness in withstanding severe winters. It is a beautiful salmon-pink and of lively habit.

Golden Rudd. This fish has striking colouring, being dark copper gold above and silvery beneath, the fins and tail being bright scarlet. The older the fish, the more intense the colours.

Golden Tench. A lovely old gold in colour and beautifully marked in black or rich chocolate spots.

Hi-Goi (Japanese Gold Carp). The gold colouring is softer than that of the common goldfish, and also the scales are much smaller.

o **King, or Mirror Carp.** This is easily distinguished by bands and groups of mirror-like scales on an otherwise smooth skin.

o **Sunfish.** Is a favourite because of its tameness, as well as its lovely gold colouring.

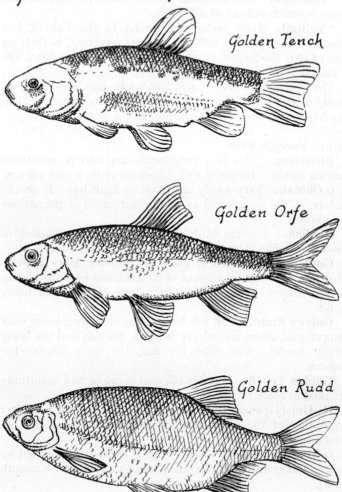

Golden varieties of Native Fish

Golden Tench

Golden Orfe

Golden Rudd

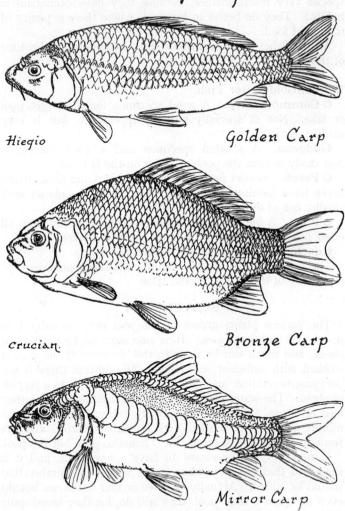

Varieties of Carp

Hieqio

Golden Carp

Crucian.

Bronze Carp

Mirror Carp

F*

The fishes marked O should not be in small pools with any species very much smaller, because they have cannabalistic habits ! They do better in big pools where there is plenty of room and food.

All the fishes so far mentioned may be bought at any time of the year.

British Cold-water Fish.

O **Common Carp.** A good specimen for the larger pool or lake. Not of specially striking appearance, but is very easily tamed.

Gudgeon. A spotted specimen and a good scavenger. Not easily seen in the pool, as it lies on the bottom.

O **Perch.** Scarlet fins, golden brown sides and dark stripes make for a handsome fish, but it should not be placed with smaller fish of other kinds.

O **Pike.** A big fish and should be kept separately from all other fish except, perhaps, in large ponds and lakes.

Roach. A common fish for pools and aquaria.

The fishes marked O are " cannibals " and should be kept separately or in large pools and lakes.

SCAVENGERS

The various plants grown in the pool may be subject to insect pests and diseases. It is necessary to keep these in check, and much can be done in this direction if the pool is stocked with sufficient scavengers. In addition there is the decaying vegetation, and there may be a tendency to a surplus of algae. The water snails will prevent trouble here, for they feed on these. The mussels actually extract from the water minute particles of animal and vegetable matter, and are sometimes called as a result, the " housekeepers " of the pool.

It may only be necessary to have a few snails, and it is suggested that one per gallon is the maximum number that should be added. Actually, if three or four dozen are bought even for quite a large pool, they will do, for they breed quite freely.

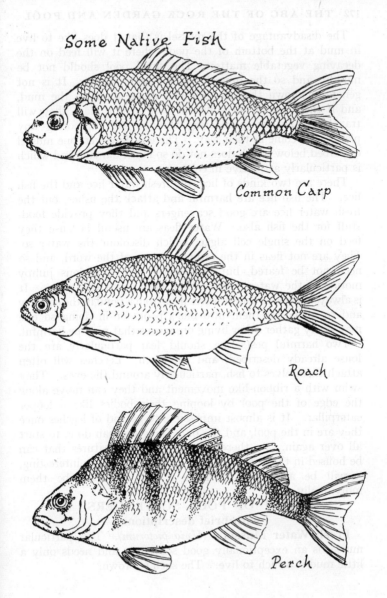

Some Native Fish

Common Carp

Roach

Perch

The disadvantage of the mussel is that it does like to live in mud at the bottom of the pool, where it will feed on the decaying vegetable matter. The small pool should not be muddy, and so the mussel will die and putrefy. It is not generally known that mussels will move about in the mud, and if they cannot get sufficient food at one place they will travel to another, blundering through and uprooting any plants that come in their way. There is, however, one mussel described below which does not do so much damage and which is particularly attractive in colour.

There are two kinds of lice, the fresh water lice and the fish lice. The fish lice are harmful and attack the fishes, but the fresh water lice are good scavengers and they provide food-stuff for the fish also. Water fleas are useful because they feed on the single cell algae, which discolour the water so. They are not fleas in the ordinary sense of the word, and so need not be feared, but they move with a curious jumpy motion in the water, and so have been given this name. It is always unwise to collect water fleas from a pond in the country and to introduce them into one's pool, for in doing so one may easily gather other living organisms that may be harmful.

Two harmful pests one should fear particularly are the louse already described, and the leech. Leeches will often attach themselves to fish, particularly around the eyes. They swim with a ribbon-like movement and they can move along the edge of the pool by looping their bodies like a looper caterpillar. It is almost impossible to get rid of leeches once they are in the pool, and the only thing one can do is to start all over again. As there are many water creatures that can be housed in the pool, and most of them are rather interesting, it will be advisable to make a list and describe them individually.

LIST OF POOL SCAVENGERS
with brief descriptions

Fresh Water Mussel. (*Unio pictorum*). This particular mussel is an exceptionally good scavenger and needs only a little mud in which to live. The shell is brown.

Fresh Water Louse. (*Asellus aquaticus*). A grand scavenger and provides good food for the fish. This species is harmless to fish, and should not be confused with the Fish Louse which attacks the fish themselves.

Fresh Water Shrimp. (*Gammarus pulex*). Resembles a sea-shrimp. A good scavenger and excellent fish-food.

Fresh Water Whelk. (*Limnaea auricularia stagnalis*). A handsome type of snail which feeds on decaying animal matter. Scavenges well and breeds prolifically. In fact, there is some danger cf the pond becoming over-populated with whelks, unless they can be controlled.

Fresh Water Winkle. (*Paludina vivipara*). Looks like a snail, with brown bands. The youngsters are born alive and are sometimes $\frac{1}{4}$ inch long when they appear. A useful scavenger.

Ramshorn Snail. (*Planorbis corneus*). Probably the best scavenging snail, as it feeds entirely on decayed animal and vegetable matter.

Ramshorn Snail. (*Planorbis corneus rubra*). A type which has a crimson body and a reddish shell. Really most showy.

Water Tortoise. (*Emys orbcularis*). This is harmless to fish but it needs plenty of room. Feeds on worms and garden insects.

NON-SCAVENGERS
but are useful members of pond communities

Newt. (*Triton vulgaris*). Feeds on all kinds of insect larvae and may also be given finely chopped meat and baby worms. A suitable inhabitant for the small pool.

Water Fleas. (*Daphnia*). Tiny little creatures which dart about in a jumpy manner in the water. They are excellent live food for all aquatic animals.

Mayfly Larvae. (*Ephemeria vulgata*). This is excellent food for all kinds of fish and so should be encouraged in every pool. May be bought from aquatic specialists.

CHAPTER XVII

WHAT SHALL I BUY?

I am often asked—how much ?
—what ?
—how many ?
—what size ?
—what colour ?
Here I try and answer !

PEOPLE often ask me what they should buy for a particular sized pool. I have then, for this reason, chosen pools of four different sizes and have given in detail exactly what might be bought under the circumstances in each case. Of course, tastes differ—but the information given does give a line on numbers.

1. *A round pool 6 feet in diameter and 2 feet deep in the middle.*

Plants :   One pink lily in the middle. Around it, Anacharis, Apium, Ceratophyllum, Elodea crispa, Hottonia palustris. 3 of each plant.

Mollusca : 36 Planorbis corneus.

Fish :   Golden and Silver Rudd, and Goldfish. 4 each of the three species, each 2–3 inches long.
One can of natural foods.

2. *A rectangular pool 10 feet long and 4 feet wide. 2½ feet deep at one end, sloping to 1½ feet at the other.*

Plants for the deep end :

6 of each plant. Hottonia, Myriophyllum, Oenanthe, one pink and one white lily.

for the shallow end :

4 of each plant. Acorus, Alisma plantago, Butomus.

Mollusca : 48 Planorbis corneus.

Fish :   Goldfish, Golden Orfe, Silver Rudd. 3 each of the four species, each 4–6 inches long.
One large can of natural foods.

3. *A larger pool, say,* 15 *feet by* 8 *feet,* 3 *feet deep in the centre, sloping to* 2 *feet at one end and* 1 *foot at the other.*

Plants for the middle :

> 6 of each plant. Elodea crispa, Sium, Oenanthe.

> **for the 2 feet end :**
>> 4 of each plant. Iris pseudacorus, Sparganium ramosum, Typha latifolia.

> **for the 1 foot end :**
>> 4 of each plant. Alisma, Butomus umbellatus, Lythrum salicaria.

Lilies, for the middle : Deep crimson lily.

> **for the 2 feet end :** Yellow lily.

> **for the 1 foot end :** White lily.

Fish : 6 each of 4 species of fish 5-6 inches long.

4. *Tub* 30 *inches across and* 18 *inches deep.*

Plants : One Pigmy yellow lily with Alisma natans, Aponogeton distachyon, Hottonia palustris. 2 of each kind.

Mollusca : 24 snails.

Fish : 2 each of 4 species of fishes, 2 inches long.

CHAPTER XVIII

HEALTH IN THE POOL

My Medicine Chest is full.   Ready for—
1. Fish, like plants, have enemies.
2. Enemies must be controlled.
3. There are diseases too.
4. What shall I do about them all ?
5. When ?

UNFORTUNATELY, fishes are attacked by pests and diseases just in the same way as are human beings, animals and plants. You can usually tell when a fish is healthy, for it carries its back fin erect and its tail fully expanded. If you see a fish swimming sluggishly or moping in some corner, then you may suspect trouble.

In the ordinary way a fish can be put right by giving it a dose of Epsom salts. Some crystals should be thrown in at the regular feeding time instead of the food. The fish gobble them up and the day or so's fasting does them no harm at all.

ENEMIES

In Chapter XVI, mention has already been made of the enemies of fish. These may live on the fish and so weaken it. The most common perhaps is the louse.

FISH LOUSE. *Argulus foliacens.* This is a parasite which may be the size of a pin's head and up to $\frac{1}{4}$ inch long. Each louse is flattened, transparent and has four pairs of legs and two little, bold black eyes. The louse attaches itself to the fish and sucks and so debilitates its host. Once debilitated the fish is subject to attacks of other pests and diseases.

Control. There is no satisfactory method of control. Once lice have infested the pool, all that can be done is to empty out the whole pool and clean it thoroughly. It is a great mistake to introduce sticklebacks or other fish from wayside ponds, as this is the most common method of introducing this nuisance.

LEECHES. There are all kinds of leeches, some 3 inches in length and some small and vicious. Unfortunately, the smaller ones often curl themselves up into an insignificant ball and so may be introduced into the pool in this way. The mouth is really a circular sucking disc, and the insect has horny teeth. The leeches can be seen swimming about with a wavy movement (see page 172).

Control. Cut off any leeches seen on the fish as close as possible and clean out the pool and start again.

N.B.—There is a creature rather like a leech known as a Planaria which may cover the underside of a water lily leaf. This is not harmful. It can be distinguished from the ordinary leech by the fact that it is in one piece and not segmented and that it has no sucking disc.

HYDRA. When feeding the inhabitants of a pool with live insects, sometimes Hydra are introduced because they can form themselves into a little circular bag. They have been likened to baby anemones or tiny octopuses. They do little harm to big fish but they do consume the babies and large numbers of water fleas.

Control. Clean out the pool. Be very careful when carrying out live feeding.

SELF-VISITING ENEMIES

Some pests are most difficult to keep out of the pool because they fly from other gardens and may just pay a passing call or become permanent unwanted visitors. Take, for instance, the Water Beetle and the Water Bug which even if they only visit the pool for an hour or so may lay their eggs, and then a large number of " maggots " will hatch out. These beetles will go on living in the pool and will prey on the pond life one wishes to keep.

WATER BEETLE. *Dytiscus marginalis.* Feeds on other insect life, so does its larva which is about 1½ inches long and of a dirty yellow colour. The beetle is dark brown with a little yellow edge, the underside of the body being lighter. These beetles have been known to attack even quite large fish.

Control. It is possible, by using a small shrimping net, to lie down beside the pool on a sunny day, and when the beetles come to the surface for air they may be scooped up and killed.

WATER BUG. *Notonecta* and *Corixa*. The former is the water boatman, a fascinating creature whose rear limbs when in use look like oars. It swims actually on its back. The Corixa, on the other hand, is similar, but it swims the right way up.

Control. As for Water Beetle.

DRAGON FLY. The larva of the large dragon fly is a dirty grey colour with six legs and a forked tail. The mouth has a pair of false jaws which cover the face and so are called by some people a mask. The larva attacks the fish by clasping it with its jaws.

Control. Try to prevent the dragon fly from visiting the pond in the day time and catch any larvae you can see.

DISEASES

Unfortunately, there are several diseases to which fish are liable.

BLADDER TROUBLE. The fish will behave in a most extraordinary manner. It will roll about in the water, sink to the bottom and rise to the top, swim erratically and shiver and shake.

Control. Give a stimulating bath as on page 180, only see that the water is so shallow that it only just covers the dorsal fin of the fish when stretched out fully. Add to the bath a teaspoonful of Epsom salts per gallon of water, and try to keep the temperature round about 60 degrees F. As in the case of congestion, gradually increase the temperature of the water if necessary.

CONGESTION. The fish will become slow moving and the fins will be depressed and blood blotches may be seen on the fins and about the body. The fish may lose colour and the gills may be inflamed. It has been likened to pneumonia in human beings and is often caused through moving the fish from one pool to another where the temperature is lower. Congestion will be brought about by sudden changes of temperature.

Control. Give the fish a stimulating bath as on page 180. The temperature of the water should be about 55 degrees F. Should the outside water be well below this, successive baths should be given day by day, the temperature of the water being increased slightly each time.

CONSTIPATION. When the droppings of the fish seem to hang from it and not to fall away naturally, then constipation may be feared.

Control. Immediately start giving some live food. Add ½ ounce of Epsom salts per 5 gallons of water.

SHOCK. Many fish suffer from shock, especially if children worry them by poking in the pool with sticks, if they are badly handled with trying to net them, or even if there is quite a mild explosion in the vicinity. Fish will leap out of the water, and they will lie on the surface as if dead, or will extend their gills and make their fins taut and turn over. Such symptoms have happened after extraordinarily thundery weather.

Control. Put two or three drops of brandy or sal volatile down the throat of the fish and place in a stimulating bath (see page 180).

TAIL AND FIN ROT. A bacterium infects the tail or fin and a rotting takes place.

Control. When the rotting is bad, cut the diseased parts of the fins away using a razor blade and placing the stump on the edge of a table. Then paint the stump with Friar's Balsam and keep the treated area above the water until it dries. In time the fin will grow again.

In mild cases, dip the affected parts into turpentine for ten seconds and then into hydrogen peroxide for ten seconds, or it is possible instead to paint the affected parts with a camel hair brush. Wash away the two solutions with fresh warm water afterwards. Make certain that neither the peroxide nor the turpentine gets into the gills or eyes. If the fish can be held in a piece of wet netting with the head and gills just below the surface of the water during the treatment, they will not suffer as much as if they are taken right out of the water.

WHITE FUNGUS. A white fuzzy looking growth appears on the fins and spreads all over the body to the gills, where it proves fatal.

Control. Take the fish out of the pool directly they show signs of infection and put them in a basin of fresh water, adding 1 ounce of table salt to every gallon. Let the fish remain there until they show signs of distress and then remove and place in fresh water. All other fish that have been in contact with infection, should be placed in a bowl of water coloured deep pink with permanganate of potash. Again these are left there until they show signs of distress and they may then be kept in quarantine for a week or two to see if they show signs of the disease or not.

Experts use boriodide of phenyl at the rate of 5 drops per gallon of water and they change the water every twelve hours. When changing water, it is always necessary to be certain that the temperature is exactly the same. In the winter the treatment may be given with water at a higher temperature, but this ought to be done gradually, and then when the fish is cured, the water should be changed gradually again to colder water before the fish is put back into the pool. It is always wise to use a net when removing fish from one bath to another, for catching fish in one's hand does more harm than the disease.

After the fish has convalesced, it may be rather weak and so a stimulating bath should be given. Eight drops of sweet spirit of nitre and eight drops of ammonia should be placed in the bowl per gallon of water. This invigorating bath should last twenty-four hours. In ordinary cases, one bath of this kind is sufficient, but where fish are very, very weak, three may be necessary. Such treatment gives increased appetite, helps respiration and accelerates the blood circulation.

FUNGUS diseases may begin through careless handling and bruising through the attacks of other creatures in the pool, and through improper living conditions. The spores may be there the whole time, but they can only attack the weakly or wounded fish.

WHITE SPOT. This is really a parasite which enters the outer skin of a fish and feeds on the blood. A colony is thus raised and it is then that tiny white spots will be seen on the fins and the body of the fish.

Control. It is a much easier disease to control in the aquarium than the pool. Fish should be removed from the pool and put into a temporary bowl so that the parasites can be starved—this should happen within a week. Affected fish may be isolated, and after two days may be removed and laid very carefully on a soft cloth, and the affected parts should be painted with a strong solution of bicarbonate of soda. This should then be washed off with clean water at a temperature of 60 degrees F., but this must be poured away from the gills and not towards them. The fish should now be returned to a bowl of clean water into which 8 drops of ammonia have been placed per gallon. This painting should be carried out once a day for four days and the cure should then be complete.

CHAPTER XIX

LIST OF PLANTS TO GROW
IN A POOL

Just lists.   NO !
1. Here we can spread ourselves.
2. Learn lots more names.
3. Become very choosy.
4. Have great fun.
5. Really learn a lot.

ACORUS.   A hardy herbaceous, water-loving plant.   They are best grown in shallow water or moist loamy soil.

> **A. Calamus.** (Sweet Flag or Bee Wort).   Height 2–3 feet.   Broad strap-like leaves.   Greenish flowers. Aromatic.

> **A. Calamus var. variegatus.**   Grassy foliage is cream and yellow.   Less aromatic.

> **A. gramineus.**   Dwarfer and slenderer variety, 8–12 inches in height.   Grows in very shallow water or at the water edge.

> **A. gramineus var. variegatus.**   Foliage freely suffused with and striped with yellow.

ALISMA. (Water Plantain).   Whorls of pinky white flowers and plantain-like leaves.   Height 2–3 feet.   Grows by margins of rivers, lakes and ponds.   As they reproduce themselves very easily by seed, the dead flower-heads should be removed. Flowers in summer.

> **A. lanceolatum.**   12–18 inches.   Slender spear-like leaves and pinky white flowers.

> **A. natans.** (*Elisma natans*).   Oval leaves, 1 inch long. Small, three-petalled flowers, white, which float on surface.   Plant in shallow water.

> **A. plantago-aquatica.**   British species.   Large stalked leaves.   Spikes of delicate rose coloured flowers.   2–3 feet.   Flowers in summer.

A. ranunculoides. Grows in bogs or water up to 1 foot in depth. Small, mauvish flowers in May to September. Dwarf.

ANACHARIS. See Elodea.

ANTHEMIS. (Chamomile). Hardy annual. Upright habit. Narrow leaves and small flowers in June.

A. cotula. Tufts of lanceolate leaves. Small, double, yellow flowers. Annual but seeds itself yearly. Wet soil or shallow water. 10 inches.

APIUM. (Marshwort). The foliage is submerged and the flowers are just above the surface. The leaves are finely dissected and spread out fan-like in the water. Plant in shallow water.

A. inundatum. (Lesser Apium). For winter and spring planting. Later in the year, the slender stem and leaves appear above the surface. The white flowers are borne above the surface.

A. nudiflorum. Oxygenator for ponds and pools. Submerged foliage is deep green. Snow white flowers. Good protection for fish in large pools.

APONOGETON. Spikes of sweet scented flowers emerging from among flat, floating leaves. Flowers in April and October.

A. distachyon. Large racemes of white, V-shaped flowers with black anthers. Oval leaves. Scent like May blossom.

A. distachyon var. aldenhamis. Improvement on the type. Larger and stouter flowers. Foliage flushed bronze purple.

ASTILBE. A member of the Saxifrage family. Useful bog and waterside plant, similar in appearance to Spiraea. Flowers are crimson, pink, or white, in summer.

A. Arendsii. Includes named varieties.

Betsy Cuperus. Pink and white. 2½ feet.

Bremen. Salmon red. 2½ feet.

Fanal. Brilliant red. 2½ feet.

Granat. Dark crimson. 3½ feet.

Gunther. Bright pink. 3 feet.

King Albert. White. 6–7 feet.

Silver Sheaf. Silvery white. 3 feet.

A. Davidii. Chinese species with coarsely-cut leaves. Rosy purple flowers sometimes 2 feet long. Height 4–6 feet.

A. chinensis pumila. Erect flower-spikes, lilac rose. Dwarf habit. 1 foot.

AZOLLA. (Fairy Moss). Floats on the surface like a moss-green carpet. Before dying down in the autumn, the foliage goes red brown. Reproduces itself yearly. It is not recommended for small ponds, as it spreads so rapidly as to become a possible nuisance.

A. caroliniana. Fronds are ½–1 inch in length, of a lacy texture. They are first, pale green and later red.

BRAZENIA. An interesting species, but difficult to establish.

B. Schreberi. Small, oval floating leaves. Flowers are about ½ inch across, purple. Will grow in 4–6 feet of water.

BUTOMUS. (Flowering Rush).

B. umbellatus. Grows in 2–6 inches of water, and is 2–4 feet tall. Handsome clusters of rose pink flowers. Sword-like leaves, which are purple bronze when young and then turning green.

CALLA. (Bog Arum).

C. palustris. 9 inches in height and prefers shallow water or the water edge. Heart-shaped leaves. May not flower the first year, but the small, arum-like flowers are followed by clusters of red berries.

CALLITRICHE. (Starwort). Vivid green foliage, very dainty and star-tipped.

C. aquatica. Good oxygenator for indoor aquaria as well as for ponds, etc.

C. autumnalis. A suitable oxygenator for outside only.

CALOPOGON. A bog orchid needing a moist and shady

position. Should be disturbed as little as possible. Height 12–18 inches.

C. pulchellus. Crimson purple flowers with yellow, orange and purple hairs on lip. Flowers June–July.

CALTHA. (Marsh Marigold). Flowers early.

C. palustris. Common Marsh Marigold. 9–15 inches. Flowers resemble large buttercups. Grows in wet soil by water.

C. palustris var. alba. White flowers.

C. monstrosa plena. Double flowers, deep yellow, should be better known.

C. polypetala. 2–3 feet. Dark green leaves 10–12 inches across. Large, golden flowers 3 inches across. Spreads very easily.

CAREX. (Sedge Grass). 15 inches in height. Grass-like perennials to grow at the water edge or in wet soil.

C. riparia Bowles' Golden. 15 inches. Rich golden yellow foliage.

C. paludosa. A shorter species. Bluish-green leaves and brownish black flower spikes. Hardy and decorative.

C. pendula. Broad, grassy leaves and long, drooping spikes of brown flowers. 4–5 feet.

CEPHALANTHERA. (Helleborine). Bog orchid bearing purple and white flowers in May.

CERATOPHYLLUM. (Hornwort). Bristle-like leaves which are submerged. Will grow in very deep water. Requires careful handling, as is rather brittle.

C. demersum. Small species but may grow to 1–2 feet, according to conditions. The flowers are inconspicuous but the fruit is horned, hence the name.

C. submersum. Paler than the above and the fruit is less horned.

CYPERUS. (Umbrella Grass). A sedge-like plant. Likes shallow water.

C. longus. Tufts of grass-like foliage ending in plumes of reddish brown.

C. paramentis. Thin foliage and similar in appearance to above, with stouter stems.

C. vegetus. Broad, grass-like foliage, mahogany coloured plumes. Hardy and in character throughout the winter.

CYPRIPEDIUM. Some members of this orchidaceous group are suitable for water gardening. They like a very moist soil with peat, or chopped sphagnum moss incorporated, or leaf-mould.

C. acaule. (Lady's Slipper Orchid). Purply rose flower on a single stem 10 inches in height.

C. spectabile. (Moccasin Orchid). A very hardy and beautiful orchid. Each stem bears 1–3 flowers of bright rose or crimson. Prefers shade, and is 15–24 inches in height.

DIONÆA MUSCIPULA. (Venus' Fly Trap). Insectivorous plant. Flowerless, but has two lobes which are teethed. When an insect settles on a lobe, it is soon caught between the teeth, and digested by the plant. Later the lobes reopen to release the remains of the victim. The plant is not hardy and should be grown in full sun on wet soil which has peat, leaf-mould, or chopped sphagnum moss in it.

DODECATHEON. (American Cowslip). A member of the Primula family, it likes waterside or boggy situations. Spring flowering. Has rosettes of narrow leaves, and cyclamen-like flowers.

D. frigidum. Violet coloured flowers.

D. Meadia. 18 inches in height. Clusters of drooping, magenta flowers with reflexed petals. Long, green leaves freely spotted with purple.

D. M. var. Brilliant. Improvement on the type. Deep rose crimson flowers. 15 inches.

DRACOCEPHALUM PALUSTRE. (Dragon's Head). Light green foliage, spikes of rose pink flowers in the summer. Plant in shallow water. 1 foot in height.

DROSNERA ROTUNDIFOLIA. (Sundew). Insectivorous. Traps its victims by means of a sticky fluid on its reddish leaves. Has delicate white flower.

EICHHORNEA CRASSIPES. (Floating Water Hyacinth). Stout stems running over the surface. Spikes of lavender blue flowers. Not hardy and should be wintered in a greenhouse. Each flower has a " peacock eye".

ELODEA. Dark green, spiky foliage is submerged and remains in character through the winter. The plant, an excellent oxygenator, is apt to grow rather tall, so any dead or yellow foliage should be regularly removed. Is a submerged aquatic.

> **E. canadensis.** Serrated, oval leaves, light green when
> young and darker with age.
> **E. callitrichoides.** Pea green foliage. Excellent oxy-
> genator.
> **E. crispa.** Narrow, reflexed leaves.
> **E. densa.** Stout, ascending stems with whorls of dark
> green foliage.

EPIPACTIS. This orchidaceous species should be grown in a sunny or partly shaded position in loam and humus in some form.

> **E. palustris.** Slender stems with narrow leaves and
> light purple flowers with white lip. July.

ERIOCAULON SEPTANGULARE. (Pipewort). Oxygenator for outside and indoor aquaria. Pure white flowers, clusters of leaves, creeping rootstock.

ERIOPHORUM. (Cotton Grass). Low growing plant with erect stems topped by snow white tufts. 12 inches. Grow in shallow water.

> **E. angustifolium.** The most handsome of the group.

FONTINALIS. (Willow Moss). A very attractive form of Moss. Is a submerged aquatic and prefers some shade. Thrives best in running water.

> **F. antipyretica.** Greyish green with very long branched
> stems. Very leafy and the flowers are inconspicuous.
> Very ornamental, and provides good cover for small
> aquatic life.

GLYCERIA. (Manna Grass). Perennial waterside plant. They flourish, so need to be kept under control.

G. aquatica var. variegata. Very pretty. 18–24 inches tall. The foliage is regularly striped with green, yellow, and white, and suffused with a rose tint in the autumn. Roots need to be kept in control by occasional thinning.

G. canadensis. (Rattlesnake Grass). The most handsome of the species. 2–3 feet tall.

HABENARIA PSYCODES. (Hinged Orchid). Slender, leafy stem, bright purple, sweetly scented flowers. Prefers shade and thrives best on wet, sandy peat. Summer flowering.

HIPPURIS VULGARIS. (Mare's Tail). Whorled stems with short, narrow leaves 6–9 inches in height. Grows in running water. Unusual plant.

HOTTONIA PALUSTRIS. (Water Violet). Oxygenator for outside pools and indoor aquaria. Rosettes of pea green submerged, fern-like foliage. Height above water 6–12 inches. White and lavender flowers. Grows in 4 inches to 18 inches of water.

HOUTTUYNIA CORDATA. Japanese species. Hardy perennial in this country. Wet soil or 2–4 inches of water. Blue-green leaves, red stems, small white flowers, 6–24 inches in height.

HYDROCHARIS MORSUS-RANÆ. (Frogbit). A floating aquatic. Small, kidney-shaped leaves, bright green, $1\frac{1}{2}$ inches across. Small, three petalled, white flowers. Very attractive, but snails are fond of eating the soft, spongy leaves.

HYDROCLEIS. (Water Poppy).

H. Commersoni. Foliage floats on the surface. The leaves are dark green and heart-shaped. Pale yellow, poppy-like flowers are well above the surface. Plant in 12–15 inches of water, and in a warm spot.

HYDROCOTYLE. (Marsh Pennywort).

H. vulgaris. Masses of foliage about 4 inches above water-level and whorls of pretty, white flowers. Needs to be controlled. Grow in 2–4 inches of water or mud.

HYPERICUM. (Marsh Hypericum).

H. Elodes. Close tufts of woolly foliage covered with white hairs. The terminals are of soft yellow flowers. Height 6 inches. Grow in 2–4 inches of water or mud.

INULAR HELENIUM. Likes a wet, sunny position. Is 3–5 feet tall. Large, wrinkled, oblong leaves, downy underneath. The flowers are borne on terminals, are bright yellow and 3 inches across. Not hardy and should be wintered in a frostproof house, in water. Dry off after flowering, and cut back old shoots in April.

IRIS.

I. Kaempferi. (Japanese Clematis-flowered Iris). Moist places beside pools or running water. Flowers in June–July. Height 18–30 inches.

Blue Peter. Rich china blue with a darker centre.

Brocade. Violet purple double flowers, yellow markings at base of each petal.

Crown Princess. Semi-double flowers, bright lavender blue with conspicuous central blotch of yellow.

Dancing Girl. Double white, faintly washed blue.

Dawn of Spring. Double wine red.

Mikado. Rosy crimson, white lines.

Moonlight Waves. Semi-double snow white flowers.

Morning Mist. Single snow white, yellow lined base.

Water Nymph. Large, snow white semi-double flowers with bright yellow base.

White Pearl. Broad, rounded petals of white with yellow base.

I. laevigata. Plant in wet soil or 3–4 inches of water. Height 2 feet. Rich blue flowers with golden spot on the claw. Thin and grassy foliage.

I. laevigata var. alba. White form of above.

I. laevigata var. Rose Queen. 2 feet tall. Smaller flowers of soft rose.

I. pseudacorus. (The original Fleur-de-Lys of France). Grow in shallow water or pond edge. Height 2–3 feet.

Fine in large clumps. Bright yellow flowers and sword-like leaves. May–June.

I. pseudacorus var. alba. Almost pure white.

I. pseudacorus var. variegata. Very decorative, creamy yellow leaf variations. Yellow flowers.

I. sibirica. Small, blue flowers. Green arching and tufted foliage. Very good for cut flowers. May–June.

I. sibirica var. Caesar. Violet purple flowers. Height 3 feet.

JUNCUS. (Rushes). Generally nuisances and difficult to eradicate, but the species mentioned are unusual in appearance.

J. effusis var. spiralis. 18 inch stems twisted in a curious, corkscrew manner. Grow in 3 inches of water.

J. glaucus. Slender, furrowed stems, green and glaucous.

JUSSIEUA. (Water Evening Primrose). Grows in 3–5 inches of water. Flowers and foliage are above water. Most members are not hardy, but one species given here is. Will grow in bog.

J. repens. Creeping masses of dark green foliage spreading over surface, freely studded with gold-yellow flowers. Needs to be controlled.

KNIPHOFIA. (Red Hot Poker). Perennial free-flowering species for the water side. The flowers are orange and red terminal spikes. Very bold effect.

LEMNA. (Duckweed). Ornamental and useful to aquatic life. No stems or leaves. Floats on surface. Multiplies rapidly and so should only be grown in large pools.

L. gibba. Thick Duckweed.

L. minor. Lesser Duckweed.

L. triscula. Ivy-leaved Duckweed and the best species. Good substitute for Riccia.

LIMNANTHEMUM. Member of the Gentian family. Has floating leaves and a profusion of small flowers. The roots should be confined or thinned occasionally.

L. nymphoides. 6–18 inches of water. Heart-shaped foliage, mottled and flat on the surface. The leaves

PLANTS FOR THE WATERSIDE

Trillium grandiflorum.

Primula denticulata.

Iris sibirica

Lysichitum Americanum.

are 2 inches across. The golden yellow flowers stand 2–3 inches above the water.

L. nymphoides var. Bennettii. Rich green foliage and free from discoloration.

LITORELLA. (Shoreweed). A submerged aquatic and an oxygenator.

L. lacustris. A creeping species with rush-like leaves 3 inches long. Evergreen and has small, white flowers. Interesting to the collector.

LOBELIA DORTMANNA. Grows in shallow water. Is a submerged oxygenating aquatic. Is 1–2 inches in height and has upright foliage, similar to the Litorella. Pale blue flowers, thin and wiry stems.

LUDWIGIA. Is a bog plant, but will grow under water. Very decorative foliage. Oval leaves in pairs, undersides are red, topsides green.

LYCOPUS. (Gipsywort).

L. europeus. 9–12 inches tall. Deeply cut, lanceolate leaves. Whorls of pale lilac flowers.

LYSICHITUM CAMTSCHATCENSE. Similar in appearance to the Arum, with a characteristically unpleasant odour. A really wet soil is ideal and this plant is a striking addition to the bog garden.

L. C. americanum. Yellow flowers and skunk-like smell. Huge leaves.

LYSIMACHIA.

L. nummularia. (Creeping Jenny). A good carpeting plant for the waterside. Small, rounded leaves growing in opposite pairs, which are ½–1 inch long. Bright gold cup-shaped flowers in the summer.

L. vulgaris. (Orange Loosestrife). 2 feet tall. Handsome bog plant and good for pond margins. Large heads of cup-shaped flowers (yellow).

LYTHRUM. (Loosestrife). They are ideal for masses in bog or wild gardens.

L. Salicaria. (Black Blood or Purple Loosestrife). Very showy with reddish purple blooms.

Waterlilies are attractive in the water garden.

Iris stylosa likes a dry, stony spot at the base of a wall, or will make an effective plant in a pan in the alpine house.

L. S. var. atropurpureum. Dark purple flowers and tapering, willow-like leaves.

L. S. var. Brightness. 3 feet tall. Long, branched spikes of small, pink flowers.

L. S. var. Lady Sackville. 3½ feet tall. Very popular. Vivid rose purple flowers.

L. S. var. superbum. Height 3–5 feet. Narrow, lanceolate leaves and spikes of clear rose flowers. The plant is slightly hairy all over.

MAYACA. Prostrate aquatic. The crown is covered with 3–5 inches of water. The foliage is submerged but the flowers are above the surface. Not very hardy.

M. Sellowiana. 6–9 inches. Light green mossy foliage, spangled with rosy flowers.

M. Vandelli. Also has rose flowers.

MENTHA. (Mint). Generally grown as garden plants, but one or two species are suitable for the water garden.

M. aquatica. (Water Mint). 1–4 feet tall. Egg-shaped, serrated leaves and whorls of lilac flowers. This hairy species is strongly scented.

M. canadensis. 6–24 inches in height. Lanceolate leaves 2–3 inches long and purple flowers. Sometimes used as a substitute for peppermint.

M. sylvestris. 1–2 feet. Leaves are very white on the undersides. Slender spikes of lilac flowers.

MENYANTHES. (Bog Bean).

M. trifoliata. Likes shallow water. Smooth, olive green foliage and leaves are borne in trefoils. Flowers are in clusters and are pure white within and pink on the outside. The stamens are red. The plant is of striking appearance.

MIMULUS. (Water Musk). A water-loving plant which grows in wet soil or shallow water.

M. cardinalis. Has hoary foliage and clusters of red and yellow flowers, 18 inches tall and very showy.

M. guttatus. Showy yellow flowers often marked inside with spots.

M. Hose-in-Hose. Has a double corolla ring and is of unusual appearance. Is frequently miscalled M. luteus.

M. luteus. Taller than the above and carries yellow flowers frequently spotted with red. 9–12 inches.

MISCANTHUS. (Eulalia). Tall grasses allied to Sugar Cane. Are at their best if planted singly in a moist, sunny position and in very rich, deep compost. The crowns of the variegated species should be protected with leaves in the winter.

M. saccharifer. (Hardy Sugar Cane). Vigorous Japanese species growing 6–10 feet high. Reedy stems, and spikelets of flowers.

M. s. var. variegatus. Has variegated foliage.

M. sinensis var. variegatus. Less tall. The leaves are striped longitudinally with white ; the stems being green and white, suffused with pink.

MYOSOTIS. (Forget-me-not).

M. palustris. Grows in shallow water. Light green foliage and clear blue flowers with yellow eyes.

M. p. semperflorens. Dwarf species of a neater habit than the type. Has a prolonged flowering season. 6–8 inches tall.

MYRIOPHYLLUM. (Milfoil).

M. persapinacoides. (Parrot's Feather). Not hardy enough to survive a severe winter, although it is of rampant growth. Cuttings should be taken yearly in July from the growing tip and kept in a frostproof house for the winter. The leaves are a delicate whitish green and very feathery. In the late summer, the tips of the leaves turn crimson. They must be grown in a moist place and are favourite plants for raised pools or a fountain basin.

M. spicatum. (Water Milfoil). Green bronze foliage, rather tangled in appearance. Flowers are pale green to white on thin spikes growing 3 inches out of water. When dormant, the buds are a clear red. A good oxygenator for ponds, etc.

NAJAS. (Water Nymph). Submerged aquatics, for pools, etc. Fibrous roots and brittle to handle. The foliage is whorled and narrow, and the flowers are inconspicuous.

> **N. microdon.** Branching stems with crowded whorls of very minutely toothed foliage.

NASTURTIUM. See Rorippa.

NESÆA (*Decodon*). (Swamp Loosestrife, Water Willow).

> **N. verticillatus.** Handsome, shrubby perennial. It has long wands which gracefully bend over and take root from the tip. Lanceolate leaves 2–5 inches long. Whorls of purple flowers in the axils. In the autumn, the foliage turns brilliant crimson.

NITELLA TRANSLUCENS. A good oxygenator for aquaria, but should be controlled in ponds, as is rather rampant in growth outside. Has very delicate foliage and branched, transparent stems. 18–24 inches in length.

NYMPHÆA. (Water Lily). See separate list of Water-Lilies, pp. 149–154.

ŒNANTHE. Fairly good oxygenator. Has attractive foliage.

> **Œ. fistulosa.** (Water Dropwort). Pretty, green carrot-like foliage and a submerged aquatic.

> **Œ. Phellandrium.** Grows best in still water. Deeply cut foliage. A fair oxygenator. Poisonous to cattle and stock.

> **Œ. P. fluviatilis.** Will grow in running water. The stem floats and only the flowers emerge. Fern-like foliage.

ORCHIS. Requires rich leafy soil, moist but not wet, and partial shade, unless otherwise indicated.

> **O. foliosa.** Dark green foliage. Stems 2–3 feet long with spikes of rose purple flowers, spotted white in May. Full sun when planting out.

> **O. latifolia.** 1 foot tall. Broad, blue-green foliage, lance-shaped leaves. The rose purple flowers are out in June.

ORONTIUM. (Golden Club). This will grow in 12–18 inches of water or at pond edge. The roots go down very

G*

deep, therefore a good subsoil is essential. Once established, they are very difficult to lift again.

O. aquaticum. Grows at pond edge. 12–18 inches tall, but in deep water the leaves sometimes float flat on the surface. The foliage is dark, velvety green, with silvery undersides, and so coated with wax that they are impervious to water. The flowers are early and are yellow.

OXALIS. The leaves have an acid taste.

O. natans. Grown in 3–6 inches of water. Dwarf. The foliage is glaucous and clover-like. The flowers are small and white, and they float on the surface.

PELTANDRA. (Arrow Arum). A sub-aquatic for shallow water at the pond edge. Glossy foliage. Should be grown in clumps. The flowers are like arums and have similar berries in the autumn. The flowers are known as spathes.

P. alba. White spathe 3–4 inches long followed by red berries.

P. virginica. (Green Arrow Arum). Bright green, narrow leaves 4 inches long by 3 inches to 8 inches wide. Thick, fibrous roots. Green spathes, long and tapering, never opening properly, and succeeded by green berries. Height 2½ feet. Best in swamps or shallow water.

PHRAGMITES. (Reed). Has a hedge-like growth.

P. communis. (Common Reed). 6–10 feet tall and makes good " game " cover. Broad, glossy leaves and heavy, purple or violet plumes of flowers. Often used on sandy shores on account of its " binding " quality.

P. c. var. variegata. Variegated leaves.

POA AQUATICA. (Reed Poa). Ornamental grass, like reed for shallow water and moist places in the wild garden. The flower stems are very useful for indoor decoration.

POLYGONUM. (Willow Grass). When this is planted in 1–2 feet of water, the flowers and foliage float on the surface, but in shallower water the sprays are above the surface.

P. amphibium. A popular species. Dark green foliage, oblong, turning purplish red. The rose coloured flowers are on spikes.

P. bistorta. (Snakeweed). Weedy plant for moist places in the wild garden. Height 1–2 feet. Spikes of pale pink flowers.

PONDETERIA. (Pickerel Plant). Very decorative.

P. cordata. The best blue flowered aquatic. It does not become untidy nor is it rampant in growth. Height 18–24 inches. The arum-like leaves are smooth, shining, and olive green in colour. It should be planted in mud under 3–5 inches of water at the pond edge.

POTOMOGETON. (Pondweed). A submerged aquatic. Most of the species are very weedy and of such rapid growth as to destroy choicer plants, but some others are fairly suitable for ponds and aquaria as oxygenators. Most of them seem to prefer a clay subsoil, and are brittle to handle. The foliage is attractive in appearance.

P. crispus. (Curled Pondweed). The common Pondweed. It has wavy-edged, clear leaves, 3–4 inches long and $\frac{1}{2}$ inch wide. These are massed on branching stems. The leaves are green or, in a strong light, reddish brown. This plant is specially useful to give colour in the winter. It can also be used in indoor aquaria.

P. densa. (Opposite Pondweed). The leaves are shorter than the above and the plant is more compact in form.

P. lucens. Broad, shining, and alternate leaves, tightly clasping the stems.

P. natans. (Broad Pondweed). Has attractive, floating leaves, either green or coppery red. Suitable for ponds and aquaria, but should not be introduced if it cannot be controlled, otherwise it may be rampant in growth.

P. pectinatus. (Fennel-leaved Pondweed). Slender, almost hair-like, much branched stems and foliage. Provides good cover for small fish.

P. pulsillus. (Slender Pondweed). Very narrow, almost thread-like stems and leaves. The loose spikes of brownish flowers are borne just above or just below the surface. Good oxygenator for outside or indoor.

PRIMULA. (Primrose). The members of this family are

very popular as waterside plants and provide colour in the spring. As they are of varying heights, it is best to plant groups of the taller sorts to separate the smaller varieties. Primulas require a rich, cool soil which is moist without being sodden. Therefore good drainage is needed and this will also prevent the sourness of soil that these plants dislike. Most prefer partial shade or woodlands.

P. aurantica. A dwarf Chinese species, 9 inches tall. It has reddish stems, dark green leaves, and orange red flowers in the spring. It likes partial shade.

P. Beesiana. This also is a Chinese bog primula, and produces whorls of fragrant, rosy carmine flowers in May–June. Height 2 feet.

P. bulleyana. This likes to grow near water. It has thin, papery leaves, and buff orange flowers, in June. Height 18–24 inches.

P. denticulata. (Himalayan Primrose). Coarse foliage from which emerge stems bearing globular clusters of lilac flowers in April–May. Height 1–2 feet.

P. d. var. alba. A pure white form.

P. d. var. cashmiriana. Mealy leaves and rich purple flowers with yellow centres. Height 18–24 inches.

P. d. var. Ruby. Very handsome with deep purple red flowers, and large, smooth foliage.

P. Florindae. This plant is like a giant cowslip and loves to grow in full sun. If happily established near water too, it may grow to a maximum height of 3 feet. The heart-shaped leaves are nearly as big as Marsh Marigold leaves. The flowers are in bloom in July–August.

P. japonica. This is perhaps the most popular of the bog primulas. Its appearance is very showy, and it is very hardy. The best position for this plant is massed along a waterside bank which is cool and moist and partially shaded. Tier after tier of crimson, pink, or white flowers are thrown up through May–June. There are named varieties for the colours. Height 2–3 feet.

P. pulverulata. Is similar to the above, but has mealy stems carrying whorls of rich crimson flowers. "Bartlett's Strain," a varietal group, gives other colours, i.e. apricot, buff, rose pink, and salmon. There is a long flowering season in May. This species is suitable for the lower part of rockeries as well as along the banks of streams. Height $3\frac{1}{2}$ feet.

P. p. Red Hugh. A charming variation of the type. Bright crimson flowers in May–June. Height 2 feet.

P. sikkimensis. (Himalayan Cowslip). One of the most beautiful primulas. It likes wet, boggy ground, and has rosettes of long, narrow leaves, slender stems bearing clusters of fragrant, nodding flowers of pale yellow, each bloom being about 1 inch in length and $\frac{1}{2}$ inch across. These are out in June. Height 18–24 inches.

P. Waltonii. This is known for its heads of large, pendulous flowers of deep crimson. The stems are covered with white farina, which contrasts with the pale green leaves. Is very free-flowering.

RANUNCULUS. There are different species for different growing conditions and the varieties will be given under the appropriate heading. The name is said to originate from the fact that these plants grow in places favoured by frogs.

(a). **Submerged aquatics.**

R. aquatilis. A good oxygenator. The foliage is of two types : the submerged leaves are divided into hair-like segments, whilst the upper leaves are three-leaved and floating. The flowers are small, floating, and white with yellow stamens. Will grow in shallow bogs as well as running water, and is at its best from the autumn to the spring. Very hardy.

R. delfinifolius. Bright green leaves. Quite hardy outside. The submerged leaves are similar to those of the above, but the floating leaves are about 1 inch across and cleft into linear segments. Small, yellow flowers star the water.

(b). Grown in or near water.

    R. Flammula. Similar to R. lingua, but smaller, usually less than 1 foot in height.

    R. lingua. Lanceolate foliage, undivided leaves and branching stems carrying large, yellow flowers like buttercups, with shining petals, in June to September.

    R. l. var. grandiflora. A larger size of the above.

(c). Hardy species for the waterside or bog garden.

    R. aconitifolius var. flore pleno. (Fair Maids of France and Kent). Double white flowers. Dark green leaves rather palm-like. Likes a moist spot by the waterside.

RICCIA. A floating aquatic. Not very hardy.

    R. fluitans. Has masses of pale green foliage, no flowers, and is rather moss-like in appearance.

RORIPPA. (Watercress). A submerged aquatic and a good oxygenator. This plant is edible by humans.

    R. Nasturtium aquaticum. (Common Water-cress). Dark green leaves and small, white flowers. Edible. Generally grows in running water.

RUMEX. (Dock). This plant is not specially useful, but sometimes is planted for bold effects along the waterside.

    R. hydrolapathum. (Great Water Dock). 4–6 feet tall. It has dark green, dock-like leaves which turn red in the autumn. The very large flower heads should be removed to prevent seeding.

SAGITTARIA. (Arrowhead). The name refers to the arrow-shaped leaves. Most of the plants in this group grow in 5–6 inches of water. A few are very good oxygenators, particularly in the indoor aquaria.

(a). Good oxygenators.

    S. natans. This is a very good oxygenator and is active for the greater part of the year. It has slender, grass-like leaves only a few inches tall. The flowers are in a single whorl and are white. It is not hardy but is good in the indoor aquarium.

    S. subulata. This plant is popular on account of its diminutive height, and dark green foliage which is grassy in appearance. The stronger the light, the less height it attains. Provides good cover for small fry.

(b). For growing in shallow water.

S. japonica. Erect, glossy leaves, arrow-shaped, with a conspicuous spike of white flowers with yellow centres, in the summer. It will grow in aquaria, bog garden or along the margins of lakes and pools. Height 2½ feet.

S. j. flore pleno. The double form of the above. Height 1½–2½ feet.

S. sagittifolia. 18 inches tall. Long, arrow-shaped leaves, spikes of purple centred flowers of white. The flowering season is from June onwards. It should be planted in a sunny position and makes a good marginal plant.

SARRACENIA PURPUREA. (Huntsman's Horn). A hardy plant to grow in any wet, boggy position with full sun. The soil should have a compost of peat or chopped sphagnum moss. After the planting is done, the surface must be covered with *live* sphagnum moss. The plant is of striking appearance with inflated, pitcher-like leaves which are pale green when young, and crimson later. Purple flowers arise from the base looking something like inverted umbrellas.

SAURURUS. (Lizard's Tail). A pretty, hardy aquatic to grow in 2–4 inches of water.

S. cernuus. (American Swamp Lily). 12–24 inches in height. Dense spikes of nodding, fragrant, white flowers in the summer. Bright heart-shaped foliage.

S. chinensis. 12–16 inches tall. Cylindrical spikes of yellowish white flowers. Oval leaves 4–5 inches in length.

SCIRPUS. (Bullrush). In the wild state, the Bullrush grows in marshes and on wet moors and bogs. The roots need restriction in the water garden.

S. lacustris. Has fat, dark green rushes. Height 3–8 feet. Umbels of chocolate brown flowers near the tops of the stems.

S. Tabernœmontani var. zebrinus. (Zebra Rush). A Japanese species with stems alternately green and white. Height 4–5 feet. Looks most effective when massed in shallow water.

SEDUM VILLOSUM. One of the few members of this group to grow in a bog garden. Is 3–4 inches tall. Has small, green leaves and terminals of white and rose flowers.

SENECIO CLIVORUM. 3 feet tall. A Chinese plant with large, shining leaves which are often 20 inches across. Stout stems carrying crowded heads of rich orange flowers. These bloom at intervals between July and September. Should be grown at the waterside.

SPARGANIUM. (Bur-reed). Has sword-like leaves. Will grow in 12–15 inches of water with the foliage and flowers well above the surface. This plant is not specially attractive but is good in a wild garden or as " cover " for game.

S. angustifolium. Stout, branching stems. 3–8 feet tall. Flat, grassy leaves.

S. ramosum. (Bede Sedge). Looks similar to Iris pseudacorus. Has erect, waving leaves, spiky heads of flowers, and prickly fruit.

S. simplex. Smaller than the preceding and has unbranched spikes of flowers.

STRATIOTES ALOIDES. (Water Soldier). This is a very unusual plant. It has long, tapering, serrated leaves, and flowers. It will grow either floating on the surface or attached to the bottom of the pond, or aquarium. If the plant has plenty of room to spread, it may exceed 12 inches in diameter. The flowers are floating just under the surface of the water, looking like cacti dahlias. The colours of the flowers vary with age and environment. These plants should never be *planted*, they should merely be dropped into the water and they will find their own roothold.

TRILLIUM. (Wake Robin). This plant likes moist, shady spots and thrives in a rich mould. To have a good effect, it should be deeply planted and in large clumps. The foliage has three-petalled leaves, the flowers are also three-petalled.

TRITOMA. See Kniphofia (Red Hot Poker).

TYPHA. (Reedmace). Aquatic plants with creeping rootstock and long, poker-like heads. They make a stately picture if grown in colonies. To stop Typhas from over-running the pool, they should be planted in large boxes or in specially prepared " pockets ". They will grow best under 1–6 inches of water.

    T. angustifolia. 5–10 feet tall. A very graceful plant with slender, linear leaves. The flower spikes are dark brown and monœcious (has male flowers and female flowers). In this plant, the male and female flowers are separated by several inches of stem.

    T. latifolia. (Cat o' Nine Tails). Often confused with Bullrush. The " pokers " are very attractive and do not scatter their seed until the following spring, when goldfinches may be seen clinging to the ripe heads. This species is most suitable for naturalizing in large stretches of water. Height 4–8 feet. The grassy leaves are 18–24 inches long and 1–1½ inches wide. The flowers are close, cylindrical spikes 6–9 inches in length and about 1 inch in diameter. The female flowers (light brown) are immediately above the male flowers (chocolate brown).

    T. minima. 12–18 inches tall and so very useful in small pools in the shallows. The plant has narrow, rush-like leaves and small, rusty brown flower spikes.

    T. Shuttleworthii. 3–4 feet tall. The linear leaves are slightly longer than the brown flower heads.

UTRICULARIA VULGARIS. (Bladderwort). An insectivorous plant and a floating aquatic. It has bladders which trap water-fleas, etc., and extracts their juice to assist its own growth. It is a handsome plant with thin, hair-like leaves and a few tiny, yellow flowers above the surface of the water. It can be used as an oxygenating agent both in aquaria and ponds, etc.

VALLISNERIA. It has long, tape-like leaves. A submerged aquatic and easily obtained and grown. The method of fertilization is unusual, as the male and female flowers are borne on separate plants. The latter are carried on the end of long, spiral stalks which rise to the surface ready for pollination. When the female flowers are above the water, the male flowers break off and also rise to the surface and pollination takes place. Then the spiral stems contract and the seeds are ripened under water. This plant is also a good oxygenator. It grows fairly well in sand at the bottom of the pond or aquaria but does better if there is loam under the sand.

V. spiralis. Grows in aquaria or in ponds in a sheltered spot. Light green ribbon-like foliage.

VERONICA BECCABUNGA. (Brooklime). A succulent plant, 9–12 inches tall. It has oval, glossy leaves and vivid blue flowers, and makes a good marginal or bog plant.

VILLARSIA NYMPHOIDES. A rare species with small, floating, lily-like leaves and yellow flowers. Will grow indoors or outside.

ZIZANIA. (Giant Wild Rice). An ornamental grass to grow in slow running water or at the waterside.

Z. aquatica. Is 8–9 feet tall. Broad, flat leaves, reedy stems and large panicles of flowers in the autumn. Good for feeding and protecting wildfowl. Should be grown in deep water (up to 5–6 feet in depth or on low, marshy ground which is always under water). It should not be grown in fast-running water.

Z. latifolia. Similar to above, only 3–5 feet tall.

INDEX

N.B. Readers are also referred to the following alphabetical lists which occur on the pages indicated:

Making a FISH POND?

WATERPROOFING. Spratt's "Glasol" efficiently makes new cement waterproof in under a week. Ready for use, and simply applied with a brush. In $\frac{1}{2}$ gallon tins (treats 25 square feet), 2/-, 1 gallon tin 4/-, carriage extra.

LAYERING. Spratt's Pond Compost consists of selected grits, thoroughly washed and ready for layering pond. Prevents muddying of water. 11 lb. bags, 3/- (covers 1 sq. ft. 2 inches deep). 4/4 post paid. Special price for bulk.

FEEDING THE FISH. Spratt's Pond Fish Food is unexcelled, for it provides a perfect balanced diet to meet all natural wants. In 1/- packets (post paid 1/6); also $3\frac{1}{2}$ lb. bags, 4/10 (post paid 5/9) and 7 lb. bags, 9/8 (post paid 10/11).

The above prices are as at the time this Book went to Press and are subject to alteration as conditions dictate.

SPRATT'S
POND & AQUARIUM FISH FOODS

Write for SPRATT'S 36 page book "Modern Fishkeeping" dealing with all aspects of fishkeeping in pond and aquarium, including special chapters on pond construction, with layout for typical Garden Pond, price 8d. post paid.

Price lists of Fish Foods and Aquatic Plants for Pond and Aquarium, also Accessories for cold and tropical aquariums, sent free on application to:—

SPRATT'S PATENT LTD., 41-47 BOW ROAD, LONDON, E.3